"The Object Lessons series achieves something very close to magic: the books take ordinary—even banal—objects and animate them with a rich history of invention, political struggle, science, and popular mythology. Filled with fascinating details and conveyed in sharp, accessible prose, the books make the everyday world come to life. Be warned: once you've read a few of these, you'll start walking around your house, picking up random objects, and musing aloud: 'I wonder what the story is behind this thing?'"

Steven Johnson, author of *Where Good Ideas Come From* and *How We Got to Now*

"Object Lessons describes themselves as 'short, beautiful books'; and to that, I'll say, amen. . . . If you read enough Object Lessons books, you'll fill your head with plenty of trivia to amaze and annoy your friends and loved ones—caution recommended on pontificating on the objects surrounding you. More importantly, though . . . they inspire us to take a second look at parts of the everyday that we've taken for granted. These are not so much lessons about the objects themselves, but opportunities for self-reflection and storytelling. They remind us that we are surrounded by a wondrous world, as long as we care to look."

John Warner, *The Chicago Tribune*

"In 1957 the French critic and semiotician Roland Barthes published *Mythologies*, a groundbreaking series of essays in which he analysed the popular culture of his day, from laundry detergent to the face of Greta Garbo, professional wrestling to the Citroën DS. This series of short books, Object Lessons, continues the tradition."

Melissa Harrison, *Financial Times*

"Though short, at roughly 25,000 words apiece, these books are anything but slight."

Marina Benjamin, *New Statesman*

"The Object Lessons project, edited by game theory legend Ian Bogost and cultural studies academic Christopher Schaberg, commissions short essays and small, beautiful books about everyday objects from shipping containers to toast. The Atlantic hosts a collection of 'mini object-lessons'. . . . More substantive is Bloomsbury's collection of small, gorgeously designed books that delve into their subjects in much more depth."

Cory Doctorow, *Boing Boing*

> The joy of the series . . . lies in encountering the various turns through which each of the authors has been put by his or her object. The object predominates, sits squarely center stage, directs the action. The object decides the genre, the chronology, and the limits of the study. Accordingly, the author has to take her cue from the thing she chose or that chose her. The result is a wonderfully uneven series of books, each one a thing unto itself."

Julian Yates, *Los Angeles Review of Books*

> . . . edifying and entertaining . . . perfect for slipping in a pocket and pulling out when life is on hold."

Sarah Murdoch, *Toronto Star*

> . . . a sensibility somewhere between Roland Barthes and Wes Anderson."

Simon Reynolds, author of *Retromania: Pop Culture's Addiction to Its Own Past*

OBJECT LESSONS

A book series about the hidden lives of ordinary things.

Series Editors:

Ian Bogost and Christopher Schaberg

Advisory Board:

Sara Ahmed, Jane Bennett, Jeffrey Jerome Cohen,
Johanna Drucker, Raiford Guins, Graham Harman,
renée hoogland, Pam Houston, Eileen Joy, Douglas
Kahn, Daniel Miller, Esther Milne, Timothy Morton,
Kathleen Stewart, Nigel Thrift, Rob Walker, Michele White.

In association with

BOOKS IN THE SERIES

Remote Control by Caetlin Benson-Allott
Golf Ball by Harry Brown
Driver's License by Meredith Castile
Drone by Adam Rothstein
Silence by John Biguenet
Glass by John Garrison
Phone Booth by Ariana Kelly
Refrigerator by Jonathan Rees
Waste by Brian Thill
Hotel by Joanna Walsh
Hood by Alison Kinney
Dust by Michael Marder
Shipping Container by Craig Martin
Cigarette Lighter by Jack Pendarvis
Bookshelf by Lydia Pyne
Password by Martin Paul Eve
Questionnaire by Evan Kindley
Hair by Scott Lowe
Bread by Scott Cutler Shershow
Tree by Matthew Battles
Earth by Jeffrey Jerome Cohen and Linda T. Elkins-Tanton
Traffic by Paul Josephson
Egg by Nicole Walker
Tumor by Anna Leahy
Personal Stereo by Rebecca Tuhus-Dubrow
Whale Song by Margret Grebowicz
Eye Chart by William Germano
Shopping Mall by Matthew Newton
Sock by Kim Adrian
Jet Lag by Christopher J. Lee
Veil by Rafia Zakaria
High Heel by Summer Brennan (forthcoming)
Souvenir by Rolf Potts (forthcoming)
Rust by Jean-Michel Rabaté (forthcoming)
Luggage by Susan Harlan (forthcoming)
Burger by Carol J. Adams (forthcoming)
Toilet by Matthew Alastair Pearson (forthcoming)
Blanket by Kara Thompson (forthcoming)

jet lag

CHRISTOPHER J. LEE

Bloomsbury Academic
An imprint of Bloomsbury Publishing Inc

B L O O M S B U R Y
NEW YORK · LONDON · OXFORD · NEW DELHI · SYDNEY

Bloomsbury Academic

An imprint of Bloomsbury Publishing Inc

1385 Broadway
New York
NY 10018
USA

50 Bedford Square
London
WC1B 3DP
UK

www.bloomsbury.com

First published 2017

Library of Congress Cataloging-in-Publication Data
Names: Lee, Christopher J., author.
Title: Jet lag / Christopher J. Lee.
Description: New York : Bloomsbury Academic, 2017. |
Series: Object lessons |Includes bibliographical references (p.) and index.
Identifiers: LCCN 2017006925| ISBN 9781501323225 (paperback) |
ISBN 9781501323232 (epub) | ISBN 9781501323249 (epdf)
Subjects: LCSH: Jet lag. | BISAC: SOCIAL SCIENCE /
Anthropology / Cultural. |PHILOSOPHY / Aesthetics.
Classification: LCC RC1076.J48 L44 2017 | DDC 616.9–dc23
LC record available at https://lccn.loc.gov/2017006925

ISBN: PB: 978-1-5013-2322-5
ePub: 978-1-5013-2323-2
ePDF: 978-1-5013-2324-9

Series: Object Lessons

Cover design: Alice Marwick

Typeset by Deanta Global Publishing Services, Chennai, India
Printed and bound in the United States of America

Because all investigations of Time, however sophisticated or abstract, have at their true base the human fear of mortality.

THOMAS PYNCHON, *AGAINST THE DAY* (2006)

Pity the man who was once in Time and can never be there again!

E. M. CIORAN, *THE FALL INTO TIME* (1964)

CONTENTS

INTRODUCTION: THE ESPERANTO OF JET LAG

Time present and time past
Are both perhaps present in time future,
And time future contained in time past.
If all time is eternally present
All time is unredeemable.

—T. S. ELIOT, "BURNT NORTON" (1936)

The above lines by T. S. Eliot capture a certain essence of what it means to be modern. Modern life—or *times*, as Eliot's peer Charlie Chaplin once had it—has been defined by our relationship to time. The two are inseparable. Think of classic novels by James Joyce, Virginia Woolf, or William Faulkner with their ticking clocks giving pulse to narratives framed by nothing more mundane, or complex, or digressive as the average day. Or, in a different register, consider the epochal notion of modernity itself—a historical period that is commonly accepted to have started with the political revolutions of the late eighteenth century in France, the United States, and the often overlooked case of Haiti. Each pursued the dream of a secular, democratic form of government centered on the rights of the individual. While the full attainment of such rights would remain an ongoing struggle in these countries and elsewhere through the twentieth century, these revolutions promised a fundamental rupture from a political past centered on a monarch and his or her life*time* of personal rule. The introduction of election cycles, term limits, and similar political calendars allowed for popular democracy to mandate its own routine of sovereign time. Eliot's lines do not touch upon such details of history, but, in like fashion, they exhibit a modern consciousness *about* time—its constituent elements of past, present, and future, as well as the concurrent habitation and interplay of these three parts in defining time, its internal differences, and its recurrent continuities. To be modern, put simply, is to know what time it is.

Jet lag is part of this broader historical landscape. Jet lag—that nebulous feeling of bilocation that thousands of air travelers experience every day—is a thing of complex origins and shadowy contours, a condition of unnatural acceleration. It, too, is fundamentally about time. And apart from the conspicuous fact of the enabling aircraft itself, jet lag is quintessentially modern. First published in 1936, the same year as the release of *Modern Times*, and later included in

FIGURE 0.1 *Modern Times* (1936), directed by Charlie Chaplin.

Four Quartets (1943), Eliot did not, of course, have jet lag in mind when he composed "Burnt Norton." Like psychedelic drugs and the Beatles, jet lag is a phenomenon that first burst on the scene (if with less fanfare) during the 1960s. Similar to these zeitgeists that expanded our social vocabulary, jet lag also marked a shift in popular culture, as commercial jet travel became a global presence. Yet Eliot's lines bear an uncanny resemblance to the experience of jet lag. After a trans-Atlantic flight from New York to London, one feels as if a time-future has been entered, while still inhabiting the remnants of a time-past. After experiencing the soporific effects of a pressurized inflight cabin and the unpleasant glare of prematurely bright morning sunlight, the time-present of jet lag can embody, disconcertingly, both a time-past and a time-future. Traveling from east to west, the opposite also holds true—a time-future contained in a time-past. And despite the aid of aspirin, a meditative soundtrack, or a stiff drink, any feeling of the redemption of time after a long flight, east or west, is often enough absent.

For these reasons, Eliot to my mind captures the languid, yet curiously metaphysical, character of jet lag that this book seeks to explore—our uncomfortable relationship to time, both physically and philosophically. "Jet lag" itself is a portmanteau expression, combining the phrases "jet set" and "time lag" and hence both cultural and scientific meanings. My use of "Burnt Norton" at the outset proposes that jet

FIGURE 0.2 The Beatles on tour, from *Rare and Unseen: The Beatles* (2008), directed by Chris Cowey and Paul Clark.

lag, while being a relatively recent sensation, nonetheless has a number of possible histories—not only scientific and cultural, but also philosophical and political—that precede its first diagnosis during the Age of Aquarius. Indeed, however unlikely at first glance, jet lag has, in a sense, always been with us. It has a specific modern history. But its qualities of dislocation, exhaustion, and unease touch upon deeper themes of the human condition—our relationship to technology, our relationship to our bodies, and our relationship to the passing of time. The literary journalist and restless traveler Pico Iyer has written that jet lag is "one of the great unmentionables of long-distance travel, as if not to speak of it is to help it go away."[1] But what is revealed when we *do* speak of it? What experiences, feelings, anecdotal knowledge, folk wisdom, and philosophies emerge when jet lag *is* pondered? These questions constitute the concerns of this book.

Jet lag also provides an unorthodox way of thinking about global history—as a history of emotions, a history of physiological response. Jet lag is what contemporary globalization *feels* like. I take this introduction's title from a passing comment in Don DeLillo's novel *Mao II* (1991) to highlight jet lag's unusual, untimely origins, as it were, as well as its worldliness and eclectic itineraries.[2] There is a peculiar universality to jet lag, like the language of Esperanto, being at once widely recognized and widely ignored. Still, jet lag has been an increasingly popular topic in numerous health articles and travel pieces—from WebMD, to the Huffington Post, to the *New York Times*, which hosted a travel blog entitled "Jet Lagged." A hybrid genre of journalism has gradually emerged involving health advice, explanations of technology, and reportage on trends in the airline industry in order to bridge the information gap between an ever more monopolistic airline business and a growing consumer base, both frequently at odds with one another. Patrick Smith, an airline pilot, is the best exemplar of this new form of commentary through his column "Ask the Pilot" for Salon. com, which once covered everything from turbulence, to the experience of pets in cargo holds, to whether it is possible for a commercial jet to be brought down by a shoulder-fired missile, among many serious and more fanciful questions.[3] This book is not as pragmatic. What we talk about when we talk about jet lag is concrete treatment and recovery, rather than cultural representation and meaning. We neglect what jet lag tells us about how we live. To paraphrase Susan Sontag, we do not consider jet lag as metaphor.

This book does. It seeks to avoid the requisite complaints, platitudes, and advice found in writing, posting, and tweeting about air travel, envisaging instead a new language about jet lag, a provisional philosophy about how to live with—and against—contemporary travel and the lassitude that can ensue: jet lag as a way of life, as improbable as that might sound. Jet lag is a perspective, not simply a condition. Jet lag offers a critical vantage point about ourselves. It denotes, literally and figuratively, the ever-transitory, in-between world which we regularly inhabit—temporally and spatially, but also in terms of technology and culture, economic transformation and political change. Jet lag is what the anthropologist Kathleen Stewart calls an "ordinary affect"—a social experience and public feeling, albeit an elusive, liminal one encountered with differing degrees of intensity.[4] Jet lag is a cultural moment. Indeed, with any luck, what follows intends to conjure in form as well as in substance the spirit of jet lag, by disorienting the reader through unusual connections, leaps of time and place, darker themes and enlightening insights, and perhaps the occasional delay—all with the purpose of reaching a new perspective. This book takes jet lag seriously.

In search of lost (and regained) time

But why jet lag now? And what makes jet lag an *object*? Despite its pejorative status as something to tolerate grimly and overcome quickly, jet lag has a story to tell. Or, rather, multiple stories to tell—about globalization, time and timekeeping, our enchantment with (yet precarious dependence on) technology, the acceleration of modern life, and our own biological limits. Jet lag is worth dwelling upon, as counterintuitive and unappealing as that might sound. Jet lag marks in particular a culmination, however seemingly mundane, of an enduring human struggle to conquer time through technology. Jet lag is one palpable cost of ceaseless innovation. It is a good illustration of what the critic Lauren

Berlant has defined as "cruel optimism." In her words, cruel optimism is an attachment "to compromised conditions of possibility whose realization is discovered either to be *impossible*, sheer fantasy, or *too* possible, and toxic."[5] Modern aviation possesses these divergent qualities, demonstrating at once the facility to leap through time and space in a matter of hours, yet the stark limitations, temporal and physical, of our current technological abilities. What defines cruel optimism from simple disappointment and resignation is an enduring commitment to Panglossian fantasy despite advance knowledge. This allegiance to a lurking disillusionment is motivated by an anxiety of a greater loss through refusal. Specific to air travel, our hurried existence of 24/7 restrains our capacity to resist flying. We have no option, it seems, but to consent to the fait accompli of travel exhaustion, along with obligatory flight delays, tight seating, and other forms of turbulence.

Jet lag symbolizes this promise and betrayal of modern travel. Through constant innovation airlines promise speed and efficiency. Yet they disclose consistent imperfections, whether bureaucratic, financial, or in terms of comfort. More deeply, jet lag reflects one of our longest held dreams and our inability to fulfill that dream: time travel. Many of us fly simply to get somewhere faraway. We think more spatially than temporally. Transcending time—beyond the time it takes to travel to a distant locale—is not a conscious priority. Nonetheless, jet lag is a manifestation of this desire for time travel—whether to go forward in time, or back. As such, it is indicative of the nightmarish head-trip, physical and psychological, that such travel can incur. The speed of aviation technology combined with the temporal mapping of the world into time zones have made this experience of science fiction increasingly ordinary. Though commercial travel today does not come anywhere close to the fabulous contrivances of H. G. Wells's *The Time Machine* (1895) or Terry Gilliam's *Time Bandits* (1981), the natural response of our physical bodies has made the fulfillment of this fantasy, in however mundane fashion, far less than once imagined.

Indeed, while time travel has been a persistent theme of modern literature and film, jet lag has been slighted. Chris Marker's influential short film *La Jetée* (1962), later remade and elaborated by Gilliam as *Twelve Monkeys* (1995), partly takes place at Paris's Orly Airport and employs time travel as a central plot device. But jet lag is tantalizingly absent. The novelists Don DeLillo, William Gibson, and Martin Amis have invoked jet lag as an idiom, though primarily for temporary stage setting—a physical effect symbolizing the disorientation and torpor rendered by globalization. Pico Iyer, who may well be the poet laureate of jet lag (sorry, T. S.), has granted it fuller attention as cited, amplifying its broader allegorical dimensions. In his world-weary millennial travelogue, *The Global Soul* (2000), Iyer paraphrases Amis by writing how a common condition for the post–Cold War world could be summarized as "jet lag, shell shock, paradigm shift."[6] Unlike the whimsical time travel found in *Back to the Future* (1985) or the apocalyptic version in *The*

Terminator (1984), which situates a machine future within an eschatological, messianic time frame, jet lag presents instead the unpleasant underside of moving through real-world time. It reveals the somnolent infrastructure of the frenetic state of affairs we term "globalization." Time travel is traditionally about repair. Jet lag is about disrepair. It reflects a low-grade version of time travel. Jet lag is time travel without the charisma.

This situation of cruel optimism—or hubris, to use an old-fashioned expression—returns us to a number of basic questions about what it means to be human: not only the role of technology in our lives, but our engrained propensity to travel, diurnal and nocturnal cycles of sleepiness and wakefulness, the celestial influences of sunlight and starlight, and the way time rules our lives like nothing else. We must

FIGURE 0.3 *La Jetée* (1962), directed by Chris Marker.

account for human behavior and biology. Jet lag as a social and cultural experience invokes a series of concerns that get to the heart of how compatible human technological ambition is with human physiology. Certainly the dream of human flight has recurrently confronted its capacity to produce tragic outcomes, from the Greco-Roman legend of Icarus to the Space Shuttle Challenger disaster in 1986. Jet lag is a more ordinary example that can teach us about this conundrum.

It is for this reason that jet lag is a thing in this world. It is not solely a fantasy-cum-bad dream that passes with time. Rather, it is a phenomenon that has accrued scientific, economic, cultural, and even political value. More specifically, it is, I believe, what the French sociologist Bruno Latour has named a "quasi-object"—a hybrid form between subject (society) and object (nature) that has a place in what he (rather grandly) calls "the Parliament of Things."[7] Latour's agenda centers on the limits of academic taxonomy and how modern practices of categorization can misrepresent knowledge production and the world more generally. In this instance, jet lag can be construed as something that has qualities derived from both nature and society. It can be medically defined as a temporary disjuncture between a person's inner biological clock and their temporal surroundings due to the speed of air travel. Yet it can also be understood and talked about socially as an invisible fixture of our restless world economy, in which we participate as arbiters, consumers, and travelers. Jet lag is what global *capitalism* feels like.

Taken further, jet lag has been a subject of scientific study at numerous medical schools, an issue of security for NASA, and an economic incentive for aircraft design. Jet lag is not a conventional object as such. But it retains object-like features. You cannot hold jet lag in your hand, but you can feel it. You cannot see jet lag, but it has presence, even shape. You cannot commodify and sell jet lag, but it has been monetized and profited from through fully reclining luxury seats and other inflight comforts. Jet lag has even generated a politics. Not fight-or-flight, as a psychologist might suggest, but flight-and-fight: cabin seating has created a provisional class structure in the sky. The literary critic Bill Brown once argued that everyday objects, rather than being inanimate, give definition to our lives—in his words, they enable us "to make meaning, to make or re-make ourselves, to organize our anxieties and affections, to sublimate our fears and shape our fantasies."[8] This view may seem self-evident in many cases—a flashy sports car in mid-life, for example. However, scholars have taken this perspective further to claim that objects are not just tools at the discretion of human use, but they can actively direct and impact human behavior— an interpretive method referred to as speculative realism.[9] Things are not what they used to be.

If this philosophical approach is too abstract for some passenger-readers, the point is that jet lag, too, must be grasped as something that can influence human behavior, not merely be an effect of it. Jet lag has come to have a social presence of its own—its own ontology—belonging to a broader set of conditions related to the unrestrained acceleration of contemporary life abetted by technology, even without the factor of airborne flight. The expression "social jet lag" has been coined by medical doctors and other experts to describe how contemporary life and its elements of hurried, haphazard work schedules and 24/7 access through handheld technology have disrupted ordinary sleep patterns, leading to such varied physical ailments as chronic exhaustion and obesity. There is no time zone shift as with flying, but the human-technology dynamic and its cyber-circadian effects are comparable. This widening predicament has been increasingly addressed in the public sphere through what is clinically referred to as "sleep hygiene" (techniques for better sleep) promoted by such organizations as the National Sleep Foundation. Elsewhere, Arianna Huffington has called for a "sleep revolution" that is meant to confront the "sleep deprivation crisis" that modern life has created.[10] The popularity of the adult children's book *Go the F**k to Sleep* (2011) has similarly inferred the growing preciousness of sleep, regardless of age, despite its crass delivery. Our desire for technological innovation has produced an ineluctable paradox—what was intended to improve our lives has had negative consequences. New problems have surfaced in the wake of new solutions. We face the extinction of nighttime.

Jet lag captures this contradiction. It is a progenitor of our techno-crepuscular malaise. Jet lag is an example of what Edward Tenner has called a "revenge effect"—an unintended consequence of ingenuity.[11] As such, it contributes to a collective sentiment of apprehension over what comprises healthy living today. An artifact of the 1960s, jet lag highlights a counterculture of global kinesis that forces us to think seriously about the qualities of being human in the face of our increasingly technological world, as well as deliberate the elusive, invisible machine of time itself. What makes jet lag an object, not just a condition, is time. Like other items and entities, it is subject to temporal change. "Time is so constituted that it does not resist the mind's insistence on fathoming it. Its density disappears, its warp frays, and all that is left are a few shreds with which the analyst must be satisfied," wrote the French-Romanian philosopher (and noted insomniac) E. M. Cioran in his characteristically hermetic book *The Fall into Time* published in 1964, the same decade as jet lag. "This is because time is not made to be known, but lived; to examine, to explore time is to debase it, to transform it into an object. He who does so will ultimately treat himself the same way."[12] Taking jet lag seriously, then, not only permits consideration of its constituent elements and its status as an object of inquiry. It also opens a door into our own object-hood through our mutual habits of modern living with time, technology, and the human body itself.

Beings and time

Among the most popular renditions of jet lag in recent memory is Sofia Coppola's *Lost in Translation* (2003), a film about a newly married college graduate and an older, jaded actor who start an improbable relationship while staying at the same hotel in present-day Tokyo. The plot is threadbare, and much of the humor is riddled with caricatures of Japanese society. The redemptive charm of the film derives from the chemistry between Charlotte (Scarlett Johansson) and Bob (Bill Murray), who find themselves unable to sleep and soon embark on a series of misadventures involving banter in a hotel bar, a hospital visit, late night karaoke with songs by Roxy Music and Elvis Costello, and watching Federico Fellini's *La Dolce Vita* (1960) in bed. Little of this activity is serious. But the film strikes a deeper chord with its treatment of time, aging, and the disappointments that life slowly reveals. Both characters are "lost" not only in terms of cultural dislocation, but also within the life circumstances they find themselves. Being in a foreign context heightens this condition they share. Indeed, their conversations mostly mark attempts at translating these inchoate feelings to one another, and themselves. Charlotte is uncertain about her post-college prospects, while Bob maintains a resigned ambivalence about his career. Charlotte teases him about having a mid-life crisis. A neon camouflage T-shirt (turned inside out) does not help. Both evince sentiments of discontent about their respective marriages. The tension that ultimately develops between them is a conventional one— whether their blossoming relationship will consummate sexually—but this possibility is dissipated after Bob's impulsive one-night stand with the hotel bar's resident singer. An

FIGURE 0.4 *Lost in Translation* (2003), directed
by Sofia Coppola.

innocence that once existed is gone. Still, the film concludes
with Murray and Johansson's characters meeting one last time
on the street, with Murray whispering something inaudible
in Johansson's ear, provoking a smile, a tear, and mutual
understanding.

Jet lag provides the premise for Bob and Charlotte's
relationship, but time and free will constitute the great
theme of the film. Frequent shots of them sleeping in bed,
individually and together, combined with the languorous
guitars of "Sometimes" by My Bloody Valentine and "Just
Like Honey" by the Jesus and Mary Chain establish and

conclude an atmosphere of time and tempo slowed down. Jet lag creates the opportunity for their unlikely relationship to transpire by enabling an alternative, ephemeral time-space beyond the judgment of mainstream social mores. It also provides a transitory vantage point for critical self-reflection on their lives. Not only does jet lag destabilize and diminish their age difference temporarily, this condition unsettles their normal senses of self by disrupting their daily rhythms. Each character gradually finds their footing by following different orders of time. Bob dutifully keeps his prearranged schedule of filming a Suntory whiskey commercial and doing publicity to uphold his actor-celebrity status. Charlotte undertakes a more provisional journey, sightseeing alone in order to discover, rather than regain, her identity. These divergent approaches clarify their dilemmas, with Bob finding his life overly structured and constrained by his career, marriage, and a past defined by regret, whereas Charlotte has only started her adult life, with too much time and possibility on her hands. The vertigo of time she feels is portrayed through passing observations—frequent B-roll footage of nighttime Tokyo through panes of hotel glass suggest elevation and distance from the world. This theme is further underlined during a brief visit to Kyoto, when the legacy of medieval Japan is briefly juxtaposed against the modern, digital spectacle of Shibuya shown elsewhere in the film. *Lost in Translation* recalls, however fleetingly, the meditation on tradition and modernity, aging and time, meticulously unfolded in Yasujirô Ozu's classic film *Tokyo Story* (1953).

What is important here is how jet lag opens up a metaphysical ground that warrants consideration. Time imparts an awareness of time. As such, it has always been a philosophical problem. What is time? And how should one live, given the limited parameter of time between birth and death? These questions have comprised an enduring philosophical theme going back to Plato and Aristotle who compared notions of "time" and "eternity," a distinction further deliberated in Augustine's *Confessions* (397–400), which positioned humankind as subject to time while God existed in eternity, outside of time. In the modern period, a range of secular understandings has been pursued—from the dialectical historicism of Georg W. F. Hegel and Karl Marx during the nineteenth century to phenomenological senses of time examined by such twentieth-century thinkers as Henri Bergson, Martin Heidegger, and Emmanuel Levinas. Hegel and Marx worked in an epochal mode at a societal, even global, scale in such works as *Lectures on the Philosophy of History* (1837) and *The Communist Manifesto* (1848). With both writing during an age of revolutions across Europe and the Atlantic world, Hegel and Marx not only interpreted the past and present, but sought to anticipate the future. Marx's analysis of industrialization in his multivolume *Capital* (1867, 1885, 1894, 1905–1910) studied the relationship between time and ongoing technological innovation—a connection that explained the predicament of modern man, whose fate became increasingly subjected to market demands and the mechanization of labor. These aspects contributed to a broader process of dehumanization—a sentiment that, while applicable to workers, has likely crossed the mind of the jet-lagged international business traveler, too.

These formidable nineteenth-century ambitions of Hegel and Marx were challenged by philosophers who emphasized a more individual approach to time. In *Time and Free Will* (1889), Bergson alleged that time was a subjective experience that was *endured*—another feeling undoubtedly shared by today's long-distance passengers—rather than a natural phenomenon exclusive to objective scientific measurement. Time flowed between the past, present, and future, informed and shaped by memory, experience, and intuition, regardless of what time a mechanical clock said. Foreshadowing Eliot, Bergson wrote, "Every perception is already memory . . . the pure present being the invisible progress of the past gnawing into the future."[13] The German philosopher Edmund Husserl defined time in similar terms with it consisting of "retentions" (the past), "impressions" (the present), and "protentions" (the future) as discussed in his lectures later collected in *On the Phenomenology of the Consciousness of Internal Time* (1966). His former pupil Martin Heidegger, who dedicated *Being and Time* (1927) to Husserl, contended that life experience—or, to use his expression, being-in-the-world (*Dasein*)—was itself a figment of time. In his words, being present required "a calendar and a clock."[14] To live is not only to perceive time, but also to be subject to time and, ultimately, to consist of time, as accented by one's birth and unavoidable death.

These philosophical positions sketched here, like Eliot, precede jet lag. But they nonetheless capture the common sense of many weary passengers that time is not so much determined by a wristwatch as it is felt. The experience of time is a matter of individual perception, both physically and emotionally, rather than objective measurement and Newtonian analysis. A creeping feeling of dehumanization due to a dance between time and technology, echoing Marx, often accompanies jet lag's post-flight ennui. After a long red-eye flight, a person's encounter with morning can resemble something akin to Salvador Dalí's surrealist work *The Persistence of Memory* (1931) with its melting clocks, a light that betrays neither night nor day, and a mysterious horizon

FIGURE 0.5 Salvador Dalí, *The Persistence of Memory* (1931).

that unsettles one's depth perception. The time indicated on your phone or other digital device does not convey the same emotional range, let alone worldview.

In this respect, of equal interest for approaching jet lag is how different philosophers and intellectuals have addressed not simply time, but the range of moods, sentiments, and anxieties that accompany time—sleepiness, insomnia, nausea, and sloth, among them. Time is not structured by past, present, and future alone. It is also organized and defined by emotive states and cultural habits of living: how we spend time. Sleep was once perceived as conducive to madness, a time for the irrational. Francisco Goya's allegorical *The Sleep of Reason Produces Monsters* (c. 1799) is a classic example of this Enlightenment view, with its nightmarish imagery of owls and bat-like creatures attacking a man dozing at his desk. Yet wakefulness and, thus, too much consciousness could also impart insanity. Miguel de Cervantes introduces Don Quixote, the hero of his seventeenth-century novel, as a gentleman of leisure who spends much of his time reading, to the point of losing his mind and enduring many a sleepless night. "In short, our gentleman became so caught up in reading that he spent his nights reading from dusk till dawn and his days reading from sunrise to sunset," writes Cervantes, "and so with too little sleep and too much reading his brains dried up, causing him to lose his mind."[15]

Still, wakefulness and even insomnia have been valued during the modern period, comprising the only state of pure consciousness and reason. Hegel's image of the Owl

FIGURE 0.6 Francisco Goya, *The Sleep of Reason Produces Monsters* (c. 1799).

of Minerva departing at dusk—the message being that knowledge is only attained in hindsight, after the day is done—invokes this idea of remaining awake as a path to enlightenment.[16] During the twentieth century, Emmanuel

Levinas went further, calling insomnia a "vigilance without end" during which a subjective sense of time, in the absence of sleep, loses its beginning and end, approaching eternity. Insomnia tested other understandings of existence, such as Heidegger's, based on finite notions of time.[17] Yet an awareness of eternity could also prompt anxieties. Jean-Paul Sartre employed the word *nausea* in his first novel to describe the stifling unease that the irreversible passage of time can impart, as confronted by his protagonist Antoine Roquentin. In a more comic mode, Thomas Pynchon has meditated on the ethics of sloth—one of the Biblical seven deadly sins and the only one defined by time. It has an ordinary, and thus looming, presence. "Sloth is our background radiation, our easy-listening station," he writes, "it is everywhere, and no longer noticed."[18]

Insomnia, nausea, and sloth are undeniably among the more unpleasant effects of air travel. But, more significantly, these periodic musings on time and this provisional taxonomy of feelings related to time provide a framework—an ongoing philosophical tradition—for situating jet lag as an object of inquiry. Jet lag deserves inclusion among these assorted circumstances that have preoccupied a number of thinkers. These preceding observations from the past several centuries underscore the potential pedagogy of jet lag—what odd hours of fatigue and alertness can teach us about conditions of acceleration, resilience, and endurance that increasingly define our contemporary lives. Jet lag is ripe with interpretive possibility. Indeed, the affinities between jet lag and these recurrent philosophical inquiries raise broader questions about the evolving definition of time, the purpose and endpoints of modern consciousness, and the meaning of sleep as a scarce resource to be protected. We are taught to ignore jet lag—to overcome it—rather than to think seriously about what it says regarding the limits of human ambition, the perils of biological ignorance, and the socio political implications of technological exhaustion. Jet lag tells us something about the *habitus* of globalization, to use a term of the French sociologist Pierre Bourdieu—the structures, practices, and forms of agency that shape and delineate what it means to live in the global present.

Jet lag has escaped the attention of many critics and intellectuals, and understandably so one might say. It can be chalked up as being a #firstworldproblem or a #middle-classproblem. In his memoir *Skyfaring* (2015), the pilot Mark Vanhoenacker estimates that eighty percent of Americans and Britons have flown, whereas less than twenty percent of the world's total population has.[19] What follows, then, is an alternative view with, what might be called, five non-lectures or memos, in the spirit of e. e. cummings and Italo Calvino.[20] The topics at hand—time, aviation technology, chronobiology, the culture of air travel, and the politics of rest and unrest, as it were—are too immense to address comprehensively here. Instead, these essays are motivated by the uncommon anecdote and are comfortable with non-sequiturs, while also seeking breadth and depth in a recondite subject that typically resides in the corner of one's eye. This cultural biography of jet lag embraces an unlikely cross between, say, Wes Anderson and John McPhee. Consider this book a draft screenplay for an experimental documentary in the vein of Errol Morris or Werner Herzog, with a blend of voice-over and images moving an improbable narrative along.

It has been commented in numerous venues that the glamour of the jet age is over, especially after September 11, 2001, with continued anxieties over terrorism. At a more mundane level, fiscal austerity on the part of airlines through luggage fees, tight seating, and meal-less flights has equally deprived air travel of whatever residual romance it once had. Yet there is more to be learned from modern aviation than these mortal and monetary apprehensions. There is much more to jet lag than being a passing physical discomfort— "an inner devastation, an unnatural perturbation" as Roland Barthes once surmised.[21] This book regards this form of infra-modernity—it is a history of the present, and unpresent. Like travel itself, jet lag, properly understood, can bring forth a world hidden from view.

Welcome aboard.

1 THE ROMANTIC MACHINE

The greatest things to be seen, the ancients wrote, are sun, stars, water, and clouds. Here among them, of what is one thinking? I cannot remember but probably of nothing, of flying itself, the imperishability of it, the brilliance.

—JAMES SALTER, *BURNING THE DAYS* (1997)

There is a family story that a great uncle of mine, Crocker Snow, once piloted Amelia Earhart in the skies over Boston several years before her legendary trans-Atlantic solo flight. She was unknown at the time. With her reputation still unrealized, he had no opinion or notion of whom Earhart was to become. They just flew, his enthusiasms for flying and for attractive women converging fortuitously, with Earhart dropping leaflets for a charity event that season.

It is an odd bit of trivia—a detail both extraordinary, yet inconsequential. But it made for a good story about the unplanned contingencies life can deliver, touching history when you least expect it. This episode also underscores the relative brevity of time between the advent of flight and its diminution to being an ordinary experience—a few generations, nothing more. I did not know Uncle Crocker very well—he had an intimidating presence, given to silence over conversation—though I appreciated through a kind of awed respect how he was part of a first generation of pilots who started out in open-cockpit propeller planes and continued to fly up through the jet age. His first pilot's license was signed by Orville Wright, there being few senior experts on flight during the 1920s. These elements, and his uncanny resemblance to Errol Flynn, contributed to a romantic view of the past I held, conforming to a broader popular imagination about early aviation defined by figures like Earhart, Charles Lindbergh, and Antoine de Saint-Exupéry.

This romanticism about aircraft and flying continues, though it has waned over time. It explains our enduring relationship with modern aviation—a reason why we tolerate jet lag and other discomforts in the face of fiscal austerity, impersonal airline bureaucracies, and security measures that have diminished the experience of air travel. It is an evolving romance, one increasingly contentious. But the idea of human flight still grips the imagination like nothing else. We must remind ourselves why we fly. We must work against the sense of disenchantment, as Max

FIGURE 1.1 Crocker Snow, 1928

Weber might put it, produced by the modern corporate airline industry.

Jet lag cannot be fully grasped without understanding the history of aviation. It is part of the broader culture of jet lag and its technological story. I draw the expression "romantic machine" from John Tresch, a historian of nineteenth-century France, who has argued for the emergence of such machines during the Enlightenment.[1] These machines included cameras, steam engines, and assorted scientific instruments, which contrasted with "classical" machines, such as clocks, levers, and balances, by approaching nature as something that could be utilized in more complex ways through scientific understanding—neither exploited willy-nilly nor insulated from human use. Aircraft were part of this new technological phenomenon.

My own experience with air travel took off early and often. My mom, originally from New England and feeling displaced in Central Texas, made sure we journeyed from Austin to Boston every summer, partly as a matter of family, partly to escape the withering heat. Flying was a joy for me then, touching some inarticulate set of feelings, and the experience could literally be like Christmas—my sister and I often received a gift or two to unwrap once we were onboard, an unfailing maternal technique of distraction. In this quotidian way, airports constituted a place for seeking origins and enabling an act of return, not only mapping novel destinations. As a child I remember my dad once pointing out on the insignia of TWA to where he was returning—Seoul, Korea—despite the simplistic lines and crude curves that gave shape to that 1970s corporate globe logo. This childhood moment while waiting at a departure gate is not unusual. Logan, LAX, and JFK—as well as Heathrow, Charles de Gaulle, and Oliver Tambo—are the Ellis Islands of the jet age. Airports are fixtures in our personal histories; they are infrastructures for our family genealogies.

Airports are where dreams can come to fruition, a location of their starting out as well as their denouement. College educations, professional careers, marriages, and overseas military service begin and end on the curbsides of airport departures and arrivals, at the counters of ticket agents, and through the gauntlet of airport security. Airports were once, and in many cases still are, spectacles of modern architecture and global cosmopolitanism. They can serve as prestigious national symbols and, at their best, supply provocative visions of the future. More recently, they have become cautionary tales of the rise and decline of government funding—hubs like Dallas-Fort Worth, Chicago O'Hare, and New York's LaGuardia are good examples of this gradual attrition and, at times, embarrassment. As part of a trend in corporate privatization, airports have been repackaged as duty-free venues for high-end luxury brands such as Louis Vuitton, Montblanc, and Hermès. Yet they also remain locales for lingering, anachronistic stereotypes, with black shoe shine men and restroom attendants working terminals throughout the American South and South Africa. Not least, airports mark the beginnings of care-free vacations for many, but they also present legal sanctuary for those seeking political refuge and asylum. Airports both disrupt and reinforce the territorial boundaries of nation-states through internal systems of border entries and exits via passport control. However mundane, airports facilitate, and impede, this and other forms of globalization. They are displays of progress and the utopian imagination as symbolized through international mobility, high-end consumerism, and advanced technology. Yet airports are also dystopian spaces of state-lessness, exile, terrorism, and increasing dehumanization through technology.

Amid these paradoxes, stories are born. We all have accounts of travel. Travel is an intrinsic part of the romance of flight. Whether near or far, for work or for vacation, by force or by aspiration: movement is as much a feature of

FIGURE 1.2 Honolulu International Airport, March 1978.

life as settling down. My first trip of considerable length—
and presumably my first experience with jet lag—was to
Hawaii at the age of four. I have no memory of jet lag,
though I do remember arriving after dark, my photo being
taken as part of a group tour, and, after checking into our
hotel, my dad buying my sister and me ice cream from a
convenience store as we sat on a picnic table, looking out
at the moonlit surf on Waikiki Beach. This moment has left
an impression, partly due to being my first long-distance

trip, partly from the unusual hour, but also because it mapped an interstitial geography between Asia and the United States that my family would return to periodically over the years, which neither Central Texas, New England, nor Korea could provide.

Air travel has become an increasingly conspicuous means of identification. As with so many other experiences once considered personal and private, postings on Facebook and Instagram have elevated travel as an eye-catching sign of status—the shot of a wingtip through a cabin window becoming a contemporary cliché. And yet travel has arguably lost much of the possibility and depth it once had. While airlines provide certain comforts—onboard entertainment, time to read, and, above all, speed—they do not allow us to wander in the way that walking, road trips, or even train hopping permit. There are only fixed flight paths.

Rebecca Solnit has written extensively on the benefits of wandering and purposefully getting lost. Her work extends an Enlightenment tradition established by Jean-Jacques Rousseau's *Reveries of the Solitary Walker* (1782) and Henry David Thoreau's philosophical meditation "Walking" (1862) that celebrated the conjoined physical and intellectual benefits of such activity—unlikely prospects for passengers flying. For these writers, walking as a practice takes on metaphorical dimensions, embodying personal freedom and freedom of thought itself. Solnit describes in her book *The Faraway Nearby* (2013) how historical icons as different as Siddhartha

FIGURE 1.3 Mount Hood, Oregon, January 2015.

and Ernesto "Che" Guevara were classic wanderers, who profoundly benefited from and passionately shared such personal exploration. During her own youth in the American Southwest, Solnit repeated this need for self-discovery, writing, "We were exploring who we wished to become, what the world might give us, and what we might give it, and so, though we did not know it, wandering was our real work anyway."[2] In *The Sheltering Sky* (1949), his classic existential novel of Americans abroad, Paul Bowles makes a distinction between "tourists" and "travelers" with the former consisting of persons who hurry back home and the latter comprised of individuals who move from place to place over a long period of time, in search of their authentic selves. Bowles wrote from experience, with his own circumstances of movement between the United States, Europe, and North Africa resulting in his eventual residence in Tangier. But if such nomadic itineraries and rootlessness signify freedom, what moral principle, if any, do flight paths and the effect of jet lag epitomize? As a less sanguine measure of our present, we might add a third category to Bowles's provisional taxonomy: many of us now are neither tourists nor travelers, but simply passengers.

Speed to roam

Against these misgivings, why fly? Besides the romance of flight: speed. As Milan Kundera has written, "Speed is the form of ecstasy the technical revolution has bestowed on man."[3] Air travel was not the first such transformation; geography had already been conquered by steamship and train. Only time was left—to get there faster. In the nineteenth century, the speed of train travel marked a fundamental shift in perceptions of time and distance, as historian Wolfgang Schivelbusch has argued.[4] Not that this shift was greeted with universal praise. The critic Walter Benjamin noted during the 1930s how professors of medicine at the University of Erlangen, Nuremberg, warned that railway service should be discontinued, since "the rapid motion would scramble people's brains; indeed, the mere sight of these speeding trains was enough to cause people to faint."[5] Benjamin himself popularized the *flâneur*, or strolling pedestrian, as the only way to appreciate modern urban life. Yet the perception of speed is relative. A half century later, Paul Theroux groused that modern travel writing was "weakened by jet lag—an unhappy combination of fatigue and insomnia."[6] Resolved to avoid this predicament, he resorted to trains, as he recounts in his China travelogue *Riding the Iron Rooster* (1988). Italo Calvino, in a memo lecture on quickness, extends this range of perception even further, noting, "The horse as an emblem of speed, even speed of the mind, runs through the whole history of literature, heralding the entire problematics of our own technological viewpoint."[7]

Jet lag has been more a problem, than emblem, of speed. It has not yet encouraged the emergence of a similar cohort of cultural critics. But modern aviation has produced lyrical writing about the experience of flight. Though aircraft have rarely carried, so to speak, the same symbolism and narrative import as, say, the train and railway station in Leo Tolstoy's *Anna Karenina* (1878)—a notable exception being the departing plane at the end of *Casablanca* (1942)—the pursuit of flight has generated a number of writers, greater than the number of train conductor-novelists or, as yet, astronaut-poets. A genre can be identified.

William Langewiesche, a former pilot turned writer, has commented, "Mechanical wings allow us to fly, but it is with our minds that we make the sky ours."[8] Pilots and non-pilots alike have attempted this task of remaking the sky as their own, among them Beryl Markham, Chuck Yeager, and Michael Ondaatje. Antoine de Saint-Exupéry arguably is the most famous, not for his feats in the air, but for the quiet heroism and crystalline descriptions of flight in his novel *Night Flight* (1931) and his memoir *Wind, Sand and Stars* (1939). Better known today for the children's story *The Little Prince* (1943), Saint-Exupéry's prose style, life, and untimely death fixed his reputation among pilot-writers and the allegorical possibilities of modern flight that pitted man, machine, and nature against one another. His disappearance, like Earhart's, only enhanced the legend. "At Pointe de la Baumette on the southern coast of France there is a lighthouse with a tablet recording the end of St.-Exupéry. He disappeared in July 1944, his aircraft one of the many simply lost without trace in the great sweep of the war," writes James Salter, another writer and Air Force veteran, in his memoir *Burning the Days* (1997). "Blue sea of glittering beauty, the sea on which Cervantes fought and where history was born—somewhere within it lie the bones of this secular saint."[9]

The dream of flight has been a recurrent theme throughout history. It is not exclusive to the modern period. This ambition dates to the classical era with the Greek myth of Icarus being one example capturing the god-like determination, yet human limits, of this endeavor.

Civilizations in Africa, Asia, and the Americas similarly associated the sky with the divine, encouraging the human imagination to look up. Angels in Judeo-Christian belief, the use of kites in second-century BC China, and the symbolic importance of eagles, condors, and falcons in Native American cultures depict this dialog between heaven and earth. But the story of Icarus flying too close to the sun with wings of feathers and wax made by his father, the craftsman Daedalus, has become a particularly infamous tale regarding the dangers of hubris, as recounted by such poets and artists as Ovid, W. H. Auden, Pieter Bruegel, and William Carlos Williams. Despite its early origins and the situation of escape that motivated Icarus's actions, it has remained a persistent allegory about the temptations of technological innovation—the risk of self-amazement through the intoxication of scientific advances, the potency of individual genius concurrent with the blindness of human will. The myth and its lessons still endure. The problem is not simply hubris, but hubris enabled by technology—an entirely modern predicament.

The legend of Icarus also captures the specific kind of romanticism that has enveloped the history of aviation, with its blending of scientific expertise and personal resolve. The success of human flight and its achievements have depended on a close affinity between the physical laws of nature and the bold fantasies of the uncommon imagination. Leonardo da Vinci's famed drawings of flying machines or "ornithopters," drawn from Greek words for "bird" (*ornithos*) and "wing"

FIGURE 1.4 Jacob Peeter Gowy, *The Fall of Icarus* (c. 1636–38).

(*pteron*), offer a Renaissance vision of this shared endeavor between art and science, with designs that replicated the mechanics of bird flight as underscored in the title of his studies, *Codex on the Flight of Birds* (c. 1505). He was not the first person to undertake this venture. Abu'l-Quasim 'Abbas Ibn Firnas, a like-minded Andalusian polymath from North Africa, attempted human flight through the use of a glider during the ninth century—a feat duplicated (ambition and failure both) approximately two centuries later by the Benedictine monk Brother Eilmer of Malmesbury Abbey in Wiltshire, England.

Several centuries would pass before the possibility of flight fully materialized from these lively paper and graphite musings of a fifteenth-century polymath, although in a form different from that envisioned by the Italian master.

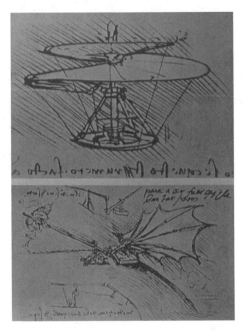

FIGURE 1.5 Leonardo da Vinci, ornithopter and wing design (c. 1485).

The European Enlightenment ushered in an era of early modern aviation, as it did other innovations of design and scientific reason, through the hot air balloon. In the summer and fall of 1783, during a period characterized by political revolutions, the Montgolfier brothers—Joseph and Étienne—launched a series of experimental balloons, with one lifting from Versailles on September 19 carrying a rooster, a duck, and a sheep named *Montauciel* ("Climb to the Sky").[10] The possibilities of balloon flight had been surmised during the seventeenth century, when the behavior of gases held particular interest in the scientific imagination. Francesco Lana de Terzi, a Jesuit mathematician at the University of Ferrara in northern Italy, had conceptualized the modern balloon—that is, using spheres filled with gas lighter than air to lift a *nave volante* ("aerial ship").[11] But the Montgolfiers and their rivals, Jacques A. C. Charles and the brothers Jean and Noël Robert, pushed this concept into reality. On November 21, 1783, with the aid of the Montgolfiers, Jean François Pilâtre de Rozier, a 26-year-old scientist, and François Laurent d'Arlandes, an infantry captain, became the first to achieve human flight in a balloon, which unsheepishly carried them across Paris, reaching a height of 3,000 feet and lasting almost twenty-five minutes. Benjamin Franklin was among those in attendance.[12]

Unsurprisingly, this new invention was soon employed for military purposes during the French Revolution, with the launch of a balloon named *l'Entreprenant* ("the Enterprise"). As the French theorist Paul Virilio has remarked elsewhere,

1ʳᵉ EXPÉRIENCE AEROSTATIQUE A ANNONAY, le 4 Juin 1783.

FIGURE 1.6 Test balloon of the Montgolfier brothers (June 1783).

"History progresses at the speed of its weapons systems."[13] Nonetheless, balloons and balloon men went boldly forth where no man had gone before, with the American Civil War witnessing their use, primarily for surveillance, as well as the Anglo-Boer South African War and other conflicts during the late nineteenth and early twentieth centuries. Thomas

FIGURE 1.7 Odilon Redon, *L'Oeil, comme un ballon bizarre se dirige vers l'infini (The Eye Like a Strange Balloon Mounts Toward Infinity)* (1882).

Pynchon has depicted these uses in his novel *Against the Day* (2006), writing how airships provided "a view from overhead" that was longed for by law enforcement battling "anarchistic murderers"—no connection to the present day intended.[14] Yet early aviation had its fanciful qualities, too. Pynchon predictably plunders this satirical potential, depicting the madcap nature of "adolescent aeronauts" during the Gilded Age.[15] His gang of hot air balloon men, the Chums of Chance, resembles not so much a group of brave pioneers as they do eccentric characters from a Robert Altman film. Pynchon's broader point, however, is that technological innovation is not always about Progress with a capital P, but can bring with it conflicting intentions and uses that spell the arrival of a new round of opportunity for malevolent forces—whether financial, state, or individual. The aspiration to fly, to attain a god-like perspective that looks down to the ground, introduced anxieties once achieved—a mood akin to Odilon Redon's *The Eye Like a Strange Balloon Mounts Toward Infinity* (1882) with its bleak temperament of airborne isolation and motionless dread, pitched uneasily between heaven and earth. Jet lag was not the first flight-induced feeling of unease.

All that is solid melts into air

On December 17, 1903, the Wright Brothers, Orville and Wilbur, flew their *Flyer* a mere twelve seconds and a distance of 120 feet, powered by a small gasoline engine, in Kitty Hawk, North Carolina. Though these measures of time and distance were paltry compared to what balloons and dirigibles had accomplished a century earlier, this event marked the next step in aviation, specifically the type of engineering imagined by da Vinci and later Sir George Cayley, a British polymath considered to be the father of aerial navigation and aeronautics. Cayley successfully flew two children and his coachman in separate engine-less gliders by the mid-1800s, a feat that demonstrated the prospect of fixed-wing design as an alternative to balloon airships and the importance of speed in attaining this possibility. There were others—Hiram Stevens Maxim, an American businessman of Maxim gun fame, came close to flight powered by steam engine in 1894, and Samuel Pierpont Langley, a former director of the Smithsonian Institution, similarly made two attempts, the second just days before the Wright Brothers' success. Reaction to the Wright Brothers' accomplishment was swift, and it was global. By 1909 Louis Blériot of France became the first to pilot a plane across the English Channel. The Russian engineer Igor Sikorsky designed the first four-engine plane with an enclosed cabin—complete with a table, seating for four, and a washroom—in 1913. The business opportunities of airplane technology were quickly being realized.

But concurrent to the early rise of airplane travel was the commercial use of airships or dirigibles, particularly in Germany, starting in 1909. The Hamburg-Amerikanische Packetfahrt A. G. was the first to use Zeppelins, named after Count Ferdinand von Zeppelin who founded the company that built them. The dirigible industry would continue for nearly three decades, providing international travel with luxury and the continued thrill of flight. It collapsed dramatically, however, after the infamous 1937 Hindenburg Disaster, in which the titular Zeppelin caught fire and crashed while attempting to land in Manchester Township,

FIGURE 1.8 Led Zeppelin, *Led Zeppelin* (1969).

New Jersey, following a trans-Atlantic flight. Indeed, to give a sense of the Zeppelin's capabilities, the Hindenburg had completed a round-trip journey to Rio de Janeiro prior to its notorious demise. Even though most passengers survived, the spectacle unfolded in striking newsreel footage circulated worldwide, resulting in a permanent end to the dirigible era. Eulogized in a song by the blues guitarist Lead Belly shortly after, it became the stuff of cultural legend for decades.

The historical conjuncture of airplane technology and the desire for distance with speed took over. Though debate exists due to factors of business longevity and flight distance, the first passenger airline of note was the St. Petersburg-Tampa Airboat Line in Florida, founded in 1913 with service in 1914. Its operations consisted of single route crossing Tampa Bay between Tampa and St. Petersburg, and it carried only one passenger.[16] After the First World War, airlines of various sorts and longevity, given uncertainties of profit, quickly took off. William Boeing, whose surname remains engrained in the airline industry today, started building aircraft during the First World War through a contract with the US Navy. By 1927 he became involved in airmail and passenger service and, eventually, Boeing Air Transport evolved into United Air Lines in 1934—a predecessor of today's global carrier. In Europe, Deutsche Luft-Reederei, a precursor to Lufthansa, was established in 1917. Deutsche Luft-Reederei had passenger service between Berlin and Weimar in the Junkers F13, the first metal-winged airliner. In Great Britain, Imperial Airways was founded in 1924 with the intention of reaching the farther ends of the British Empire. The airline that is Air France today started in 1933, while Koninklijke Luchtvaart Maatschappij voor Nederland en Koloniën (KLM) began in 1919. KLM holds the distinction of being the oldest airline continually operating under the same name. It flew as faraway as Jakarta, Indonesia, then under Dutch colonial rule—a route that took ten days, far faster than any ship.[17] Latin America, Asia, and Australia also witnessed the birth of different carriers during the same period.[18] The upshot is that the corporate landscape we are accustomed to has early beginnings, with apprehensiveness over profitability being a long-term feature of the industry.

In a partnership coinciding with Pynchon's worldview, airmail and government contracts became vital during this period, providing antecedents to Federal Express, DHL, and the business of international express mail and courier services. Though airlines had been founded, the widespread use of flight was still uncertain, with entertainment at circuses through barnstorming and various aerial stunts being the primary mode of popularization. Airmail filled this commercial vacuum. In 1918 the US Postal Service started an airmail route from New York to Washington, DC, which became known as US Air Mail Route No. 1. Connections were soon extended to Chicago and San Francisco by 1920. This coast-to-coast service took seventy-eight hours in good weather through a combination of flights and railway transport. Provisional airports were hastily built—at times consisting only of open pasture—and pilots flew exclusively during the day, using visible landmarks as a means of navigation. However, despite the advantage of speed, airmail did not initially merit its expense, with pilots soon encouraged to fly at night for greater efficiency of delivery. Given the lack of navigational instruments and techniques for measuring altitude in darkness, the dangers of this practice became readily apparent, through a number of fatal crashes. Of the forty original pilots of the US Postal Service, nineteen died within the first three years. Still, attempts at day and night service persevered with a transcontinental test flight in 1921 from San Francisco to New York resulting in mail delivered in approximately thirty-three hours and twenty minutes, cutting the time of day flying alone by more than half. Airmail had proved itself. By 1925, the Air Mail Act—also known as the Kelly Act—was passed by Congress, authorizing the expansion of airmail and encouraging the growth of commercial aviation more generally. Indeed, railroads, which had dominated transport during the Gilded Age, complained of the federal government's monopoly over aviation. The government itself found it challenging to construct a new transportation infrastructure of routes and landing strips to sustain this emergent industry.

A precursor to jet lag also took shape. The demands of on-time delivery, the unusual hours kept to maintain continual cross-country transport, and the general stress of piloting open-cockpit aircraft, exposed to the elements, produced a new and special kind of modern exhaustion. This fatigue, combined with the anxiety of constant mortal danger, was alleviated in part through federal regulation. The Air Commerce Act (1926), guided by then secretary of commerce Herbert Hoover, inaugurated a regulatory system similar to that existing for ships and maritime traffic. Private industry was urged to take on the primary burden of investing in the development of routes and air "ports" while the government would assist through formalizing licensing and meeting navigational needs—a familiar public-private political logic. As this relationship unfolded, much fanfare greeted the new airmail service as it connected towns, large and small, across the country. Local politicians gave speeches, and businessmen showcased their goods and services at landing fields. Crowds would gather to see pilots take off and land, at times in farm pasture and on other occasions by the light of bonfires, lit for navigation.

Charles Lindbergh's nonstop trans-Atlantic flight in 1927 proved to be a turning point, especially for passenger service. In 1926, an estimated 5,800 people paid to travel by air—a small, but remarkable, figure given the novelty of

FIGURE 1.9 Charles Lindbergh (1927).

flight. By 1930, the number rose to an astonishing 173,000 passengers. Amelia Earhart's parallel feat in 1932, becoming the first woman to complete a solo trans-Atlantic flight, further spurred this momentum. Passenger service became a priority, with the introduction of larger trimotor planes that could carry over a dozen passengers in an enclosed cabin. While many flights were short and often cancelled due to weather—an aggravation entirely unfamiliar to us in the present—the popularity of air travel had commenced.

Like United, a number of American carriers still in existence today materialized out of the conglomeration of different regional mail and passenger services—American Airways, later renamed American Airlines in 1934, being another example. Nurses were soon hired to attend to the comfort and needs of passengers. Ellen Church is considered the first flight "stewardess," working for Boeing on its eighteen-passenger Boeing 80A. Swissair followed suit as the first European carrier to employ women. As airlines expanded service to Africa, Asia, and the Pacific region, this era also became known for its "flying boats," which proved highly useful when airfield construction was minimal or absent. Floatplanes and seaplanes also offered a sense of safety for prolonged transoceanic flights. Pan American Airways began a trans-Pacific passenger flight as early as 1936, a year after airmail service was established between San Francisco and Manila. The trip took seven days.

It is here that an anti-romantic view of flight—its potential for destruction—should also be acknowledged. The military

FIGURE 1.10 Detail of *Guernica* from *Pablo Picasso* (1986), directed by Didier Baussy.

use of balloons was surpassed during the First World War through combat fighter planes, though the introduction of aerial bombing, which targeted civilians and normalized the notion of total war, had the most devastating long-term impact on the practice of war, lasting up to the drone warfare of the present. The 1937 bombing of Guernica by German and Italian forces aiding the fascist Franco government in Spain during the Spanish Civil War is among the most notorious instances of this new immorality. Famously depicted by Pablo Picasso in his epic 1937 painting, completed within weeks of the aerial massacre, the bombardment attracted equal attention from other artists and writers such as Alain Resnais and Paul Éluard. In an essay for the *New Yorker* that later formed part of his book *On the Natural History of Destruction* (2003), W. G. Sebald wrote of the 1943 Allied bombing campaign that targeted Hamburg, after which,

> horribly disfigured corpses lay everywhere. Bluish little phosphorus flames still flickered around many of them; others had been roasted brown or purple and reduced to a third of their normal size. They lay doubled up in pools of their own melted fat. . . . Elsewhere, clumps of flesh and bone or whole heaps of bodies had cooked in the water gushing from bursting boilers. Other victims had been so badly charred and reduced to ashes by the heat, which had risen to a thousand degrees or more, that the remains of families consisting of several people could be carried away in a single laundry basket.[19]

Sebald's meditation is not to absolve Nazi Germany or obscure its brutal history of organized genocide during the war. Rather, similar to Kurt Vonnegut and John Hersey in *Slaughterhouse-Five* (1969) and *Hiroshima* (1946), Sebald underscores the moral ambiguities of total war, when hard distinctions between combatant and civilian, friend and enemy, right and wrong can quickly dissolve—a collapse of principles expedited by the advent of modern aerial bombing. As Sven Lindqvist has described in *A History of Bombing* (2001), this technology was tested in particular

FIGURE 1.11 Kim Phúc in *Hearts and Minds* (1974), directed by Peter Davis.

on colonized and other "native" peoples of color—a fact substantiated with the Italian slaughter of Ethiopians during the Second Italo-Ethiopian War, the dropping of atomic bombs on Hiroshima and Nagasaki, the carpet bombing of Cambodia, and the indiscriminate use of napalm in Vietnam. A thin red line runs from the civilian victims of Guernica to Phan Thị Kim Phúc, the nine-year-old girl who survived an American napalm attack, iconically captured by photographer Nick Ut—a rendition of Edvard Munch's *The Scream* (1893) horrifically come to life.

These latter examples were enabled by innovations in technology. Amid early trends in aviation, the birth of jet propulsion engineering also occurred. It, too, has origins that go back to ancient Egypt and medieval China, when

FIGURE 1.12 The de Havilland DH 106 Comet.

scientists experimented with compressed gas and steam. Leaping ahead, the first proposals for airplane jet propulsion were made in the 1920s and 1930s in Great Britain and Germany. By August 1939, the first jet plane was flown in Germany—the Heinkel He 178. The Second World War encouraged the development of this new technology, with the Messerschmitt Me 262—the first fighter jet—appearing in 1944. By July 1949, the first commercial jet plane was tested—the de Havilland DH 106 Comet, a plane that at first glance looks immediately familiar, approximating the form and style of commercial aircraft we know today. It went into service in 1952, introduced by British Overseas Airways Corporation (later British Airways) with flight routes from

London to Johannesburg and London to Tokyo. Not to be outcompeted, Boeing developed the 707, which came into use by 1958, becoming the preferred commercial jet up through the 1970s, following a number of crashes of the Comet aircraft. The ascendance of American aviation—and jet lag—had begun.

Dazed and confused

Technology has a way of erasing history. It is seen and desired as a mirror of the present and future, not a faithful representation of the past. It actively spurns the antiquated. Yet this backdrop of inspired polymaths, obsolete feats of engineering, corporate aspiration, and military malfeasance is essential for grasping the origins of jet lag—and its possible futures. Jet lag is not only a momentary physiological effect. It is an outcome of innovation and Icarian ambition. It is an effect of history.

In writing this book, I have wondered if my generation—that is, Gen-Xers born during the late 1960s and 1970s—can be said to be the first to experience jet lag as an ordinary occurrence and whether it is therefore meaningful to claim this as a distinction. For sure, jet lag is an ailment that affects everyone to a degree, regardless of age, gender, race, or class, let alone generational cohort. But is there a historical purpose or cultural value to fixing this coincidence of birth, technology, and exhaustion as a particular group marker—to be "the jet lag generation"? I think there is, with implications that extend beyond jet lag itself. To associate oneself with jet lag in a historical sense is to take measure of a social shift in speed, to be conscious of the origins of the escalating pace of life in which we all find ourselves—a point to which I shall return. As the religion scholar Mark C. Taylor has argued, speed has a way of annihilating memory, not just space and time.[20] The romanticism and anti-romanticism of aviation as sketched in this memo-non-lecture provide one way of remembering how we got here, and where we might be going.

"Of so much haste, of so much impatience, our machines are the consequence and not the cause," E. M. Cioran has written in *The Fall into Time*, with regards to industrial technology and its unremitting spread. "It is not they who are driving civilized man to his doom; rather he has invented them because he was already on his way there; he sought means, auxiliaries to attain it faster and more effectively."[21] In like fashion Martin Heidegger contended in "The Question Concerning Technology" (1954), "The essence of technology is by no means anything technological. . . . Everywhere we remain unfree and chained to technology, whether we passionately affirm or deny it."[22] Technology and its innovations must not be treated as neutral. Following Cioran and Heidegger, we need to think more clearly about how we are not victims of machines and their tempos, but how we are victims of ourselves.

And yet the imagination must not be abandoned. One final image that captures this convergence of human

FIGURE 1.13 Yves Klein, *Leap into the Void* (1960).

ambition, technology, and the dream of flight is *Leap into the Void* (1960) by Yves Klein. The technology in this case is the camera, but like balloons, planes, and other aircraft it can convey the wild illusions of flight. The image—taken and edited by Harry Shunk and János Kender—depicts Klein in midair, facing what appears to be imminent injury, possibly death. It possesses a distinct sense of suicidal dread. Yet it also expresses the immediate exhilaration of flight, however temporary. It is a decisive moment, in the manner of Henri

Cartier-Bresson, though a neo-Dadaist one, playfully staged with human flight juxtaposed against the riding of a bicycle in the middle ground and a train nearly concealed in the background. Combined, Klein's artwork raises complex questions at the start of the 1960s, jet lag's first decade. Where is the joy of flight taking us? And at what cost?

2 BABEL'S CLOCK

Time is an illusion. Lunchtime doubly so.
**—DOUGLAS ADAMS, *THE HITCH HIKER'S
GUIDE TO THE GALAXY* (1979)**

A sense of time is one of our most basic traits as human beings. How we spend our days, how we think of our identities through the accumulation of experience, and how we imagine (or choose to ignore) our impending mortality—these ordinary features of life define our worldviews and how we live. It is not an exaggeration to say that the central preoccupation of our lives is how to make meaning out of the time we have. Clichéd platitudes aside, we have been acculturated to answer this question in a number of ways: educational fulfillment, gainful employment, family happiness, civic duty, and spiritual enlightenment are habitually cited as essential for spending one's lifetime properly.

However, these fundamental elements that seek a comprehensive, enduring happiness are often at risk. Our lives are broken down into personal and public calendars that structure days, months, and years that can bring either progress or ennui. The celebration of birthdays, the marking of religious and secular holidays, and annual cycles of education and career, among many activities, give shape and meaning to time in an immediate sense. We can plan at this quotidian level of time perception. Yet our terminal relationship to time—our biological mortality—is concealed, if not wholly forgotten, by this more palpable horizon of everyday life. As the urban theorist David Harvey has written, repetitive cycles give "a sense of security in a world where the general thrust of progress appears to be ever onwards and upwards into the firmament of the unknown."[1] In this way, the commonplace regularity of annual calendars and daily clocks can introduce time's more illusory qualities, whether guaranteed safety, the perpetual deferment of death, or, as Douglas Adams would have it, the promise of lunchtime.

Time is and is not an illusion. Jet lag, with its mix of technological, biological, and temporal elements, confirms this paradox. Whether time is gained or lost by air travel, there is a momentary disjuncture between how one feels and what time it is—an unreality. In this regard, what we take to be objective measurement is also socially inflected, if not wholly fabricated. Time measurement—or chronometry— has always possessed this tension, the imprint of human influence impacting scientific impartiality.

Chronometry itself is a historical formation, a product of time. The twelve-month year, for example, dates from the Roman period, originating with the Julian calendar established by Julius Caesar in 45 BC and later revised in 1582 by Pope Gregory XIII, henceforth resulting in the Gregorian calendar used today. The seven-day week has even older origins— the Judaic book of Genesis indicating one tradition—related to celestial movements first charted by Babylonian sources during the fifth century BC and later observed in Greece, Persia, India, and China. The twenty-four-hour day similarly has an ancient pedigree, but was only gradually formalized beginning in the late nineteenth century. These long-standing practices of timekeeping exhibit a history of human understanding about planetary movements, the daily rotation of the earth, and the annual orbit of the earth around the sun as observed through seasonal change—a natural celestial time that is not invented. But our perceptions of causality for such cycles, our units of measurement, and their uniform implementation have been imperfect, being subject to scientific disagreement and political discord, local cultural practices and biased economic incentives. The preference for solar calendars over lunar almanacs is but one instance of human choice in the face of an indifferent universe.

Scale is important. Amid these measurements and their meanings, the perfect clock may, in fact, be the human body. As Martin Heidegger argued, being-in-the-world "itself is the clock."[2] Jet lag appears to confirm this notion. The body does not measure time in a manner in which we are typically accustomed. But it certainly provides the most significant sense of time, however elusive, irregular, or seemingly inaccurate its timekeeping may look. We ignore it at our peril. Our bodies tell us when to eat, the optimal time for sleep, and when we are ready (or not ready) to wake up. At a different level, puberty, menopause, and the steady decline of our physical abilities are physiological conditions that alert us to the passage of time, both individually and communally. There is no illusion that aging and a biological death awaits us all. Jet lag reminds us, however momentarily, of this congenital clock that cannot be rewound.

Our repertoire of mechanical tools for timekeeping treats time differently. Though invented with purpose and undoubtedly useful, the automation of time distracts us from the rhythms and routine of our own biology and the natural world. A shared understanding exists that to know the exact hour and minute of the day by consulting a wristwatch or handheld device allows us to utilize our time, mortal and otherwise, better. Yet the difference between biological and mechanized time can easily be lost. An unspoken hierarchy often occurs between the two, with the white noise of technological innovation interrupting and obscuring what our biological clocks tell us. Indeed, consciously or unconsciously, we tend to favor mechanized time and its objective view that time is limitless, a resource without end. While we complain about *losing* time on some matters, we also have the ability to *make* time for other things, even if this prospect is a modern mirage. A cognitive dissonance can surface between this sanguine promise that feeds daily aspirations and the longer-term reality that renders this idealism as precisely that—a disjuncture of desire and experience, a cruel optimism, not unlike jet lag.

I call this chapter "Babel's Clock" to capture the long-held dream of universal time and timekeeping, yet the multiplicity of time in actual perception and practice. It speaks to the ambition of aligning our biological clocks with our social clocks as defined by families, careers, and personal goals—a discord of timekeeping that today seems ever more apart. The biblical story of the Tower of Babel is one of humankind seeking to reach heaven and, thus, divine status by building a great tower—a plan ultimately thwarted by God, who scattered humankind across the world. People, who until then shared a common tongue, were further divided by language. The notion of attaining universal time and the history of timekeeping bear similar themes of aspiration and dispersal, omniscience and incompletion. It is a dilemma that has preoccupied thinkers from Galileo to Einstein.

Jet lag is part of this chronological dream. It is not only an outcome of technological innovation, as addressed in the previous chapter. It is also the perverse product of two conflicting orders of time, mechanical and biological. This memo-non-lecture addresses the former: jet lag as an unanticipated effect of the formalization of global time since the nineteenth century. We measure and grasp jet lag through the number of time zones crossed. Yet, despite these efforts at temporal objectivity, jet lag still indicates how time remains a subjective, human-made experience. To endure jet lag is not only to feel the speed of aviation technology. It is also to encounter the modern spatial mapping of time—how time is an ineluctable infrastructure for our lives.

A briefer history of time

In the introduction, I made the assertion that to be modern is to know what time it is. Modern life has imposed a particularly acute consciousness and sensibility about time measured in hours, seconds, and even fractions of a second. "The clock, not the steam-engine, is the key machine of the modern industrial age," Lewis Mumford wrote in his classic study, *Technics and Civilization* (1934). "For every phase of its development the clock is both the outstanding fact and the typical symbol of the machine: even today no other machine is so ubiquitous."[3] This assertion during the 1930s has only been reinforced. The digitalization of our lives through online platforms such as Facebook, Twitter, and Instagram have added further structure to this ubiquity and hyper-awareness through undeviating timelines, instantaneous commentary, and the capacity to document life's moments straightaway in the universal language of photography. These new formats are not clocks per se—they are more archival in scope than attuned to temporal cycles that foretell the future—but they do constitute a method of timekeeping. Our digital selves readily evince Heidegger's perspective that being *is* time.

Yet it is also true that timekeeping has been a long-standing practice of human civilization. One of the earliest known machines—the Antikythera mechanism (c. 150–100 BC), named after the Greek island of Antikythera, the location of the shipwreck in which it was found in 1900—is believed to have computed the movement of stars and planets and, in doing so, provisionally keep track of time. So-called "cartographies of time"—that is, depictions of time in visual-spatial form through timelines, timetables, genealogical trees, and flow charts—have similarly comprised an enduring practice. Historians Anthony Grafton and Daniel Rosenberg have addressed the multiple approaches and diverse forms that such "time maps" have taken in Western culture.[4] One notable example is an illustration from Lorenz Faust's *Anatomia statuae Danielis* (1586), which utilizes the physical anatomy of the titular figure from the biblical Book of Daniel to organize and interpret events and polities, as well as envisage the future—an inventive visual intersection of history and prophecy given that the Book of Daniel concerns eschatology and apocalypse.[5] A more familiar example is the basic timeline, which today is taken for granted as a means of giving spatial form and direction to time. It is nonetheless a relatively recent technique—a tool commonly used only since the eighteenth century. Joseph Priestley's *A Chart of Biography* (1765) was among the first to depict and explain the progress of time through this idiom. However, such successful linear clarity can also be too reductive and simple. Timelines provide a suggestive visual model, not a facsimile of historical change with its multiple directions and complex plotlines.[6]

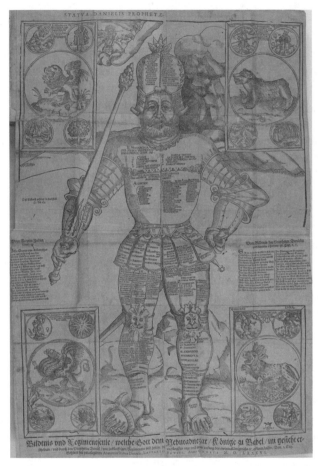

FIGURE 2.1 Lorenz Faust, illustration from *Anatomia statuae Danielis* (1586).

These flights of imagination and inventiveness from chronographers of the past indirectly comment on the relative creative impoverishment of timekeeping today—the digital clock being emblematic of our functional present. For sure, genealogical trees, flow charts, and timetables remain widely used. But precision can lead to banality. Furthermore, a distinction is needed between daily timekeeping and the quest for deeper historical understanding. "Chronologers" such as Priestley invented sequences of cause and effect that attempted to organize time to explain historical routes from the past to the present, whether through human or natural disasters, king lists, or celestial movements. On the other hand, timekeeping was and still is concerned with scheduling in relation to hours of daytime and nighttime, though this light-determined schema has faded rapidly over the past century. Clocks in the past have been closely tied to the natural world—think of sun dials, astronomical clocks, candle clocks, water clocks, and hourglasses filled with sand, each of which depends on outside stimuli (sunlight, stars, gravity) and recurrent testing to establish time dependably. The advent of mechanical clocks, beginning as early as eighth-century China and later medieval Europe, did not completely move away from nature—gravity is omnipresent—but it did augur a departure from the seasonal and celestial rhythms found in the natural world. Indeed, it marked a transition that inspired a new round of philosophical rumination over time and our subjection to it—not on eschatological grounds as theologians would have it, but rather how time could be utilized productively in more secular, everyday terms. As Mumford discusses, the medieval development of timekeeping among Benedictine monastic brotherhoods, which were known for their work ethic, indicated, "The clock is not merely a means of keeping track of the hours, but of synchronizing the actions of men."[7]

This shift coincided with the Copernican Revolution, opening a horizon of scientific thought that enabled time, celestial motion, and the natural world to be approached and understood through deductive reasoning rather than be the province of faith in divine will. This revolution was further spurred by the European "discovery" and colonization of the Americas, which confounded and ultimately transformed Western knowledge, including notions of global time. One of the great scientific pursuits during the early modern period was the determination of latitude and longitude for purposes of navigation and global timekeeping. If seemingly mundane in the present—little more than grade school knowledge of the Equator, Greenwich Mean Time, the Tropics of Cancer and Capricorn, and so forth on a classroom globe—these lines nonetheless enabled European global expansion through a more precise cartography. The idea of dividing the world into directional coordinates running north and south and east and west has ancient origins, with Ptolemy's second-century *Geography* exemplifying this early thinking. Christopher Columbus used a version of Ptolemy's original atlas thirteen hundred years later to navigate westward on his fateful voyage across the Atlantic. What was unclear, however, with Columbus being a prime example, was how to establish location, distance, and time when navigating east or west. Latitude, which determined location north or south of the Equator, could be ascertained by measuring the sun and stars in relation to the horizon—especially the North Star (Polaris), which had been used for navigation since antiquity. Longitude required a different strategy.

As Dava Sobel has written in her popular history of longitude, the measurement of how far east or west one was necessitated an accurate sense of time between one's current location and one's point of origin. Without the benefit of modern communication to verify time differences, let alone the absence of precise timekeeping itself, inaccuracies were abundant. The result was that ships got lost at sea, with many crews and their cargoes finding their fate beneath the waves. This is not to say there were no tactics to avoid such demise. Following trade winds and retracing the routes of other ships were two common methods. But these techniques proved limited with unpredictable currents and if the wind died, which left few alternatives. The shared use of shipping lanes also guaranteed piracy. Fog and overcast skies could make latitudinal navigation by the stars dire as well. And venturing into new waters only heightened such lurking dangers. In short, the search for measuring longitude preoccupied many seafaring countries, with Britain's Longitude Act of 1714, which offered a sizable monetary prize for its determination, being an example of this keenly sought goal. Longitude was not merely a scientific matter, but had vast political and economic implications, given the ambition and scale of imperial power involved. Indeed, the testing ground for longitude by law was the West Indies, where an enormous amount of financial capital had been invested in an extremely lucrative sugar industry, forcibly produced by African slaves.[8]

Early attempts had focused on astronomical observation under the rational belief that, if latitude could be ascertained by the stars, so could longitude. The Italian astronomer Galileo Galilei—who played a key role in the Copernican shift, which positioned the earth revolving around the sun rather than the opposite, as previously thought—was among those who engaged with this problem. He used the moons of Jupiter and the regularity of their orbits to construct a timetable that navigators could consult and rely upon nightly. The outward daffiness of this approach was as apparent then as it might seem now. Nevertheless, it gained acceptance after Galileo's death—specifically, the importance of celestial motion and the new ability that the invention of the telescope provided. Astronomical observatories were founded in Paris and Greenwich during the seventeenth century with the intention of mapping the universe, a project that continues today.

This celestial method to solving longitude, however, competed with an alternative—the effects of which have defined how we think of jet lag. Essentially, a separate idea was to have a mechanical clock onboard ships—a "marine chronometer"—that would keep constant track of the time in the original homeport, thus allowing for navigators to measure the difference in time between that onboard and the current time back home. Through this time difference—or time lag—sailors could determine the number of degrees east or west a ship had traveled. The trick was inventing a mechanical clock that would be dependable. Galileo once more had a posthumous hand in this history with the idea of a pendulum as the working mechanism for predictable timekeeping. But a pendulum suffered from the rocking of ships, which rendered such a mechanism unseaworthy. During the seventeenth century, the Dutch astronomer Christiaan Huygens and the English scientist Robert Hooke developed and claimed individual patent rights over a spring mechanism that circumvented the problem of the unsteady pendulum.

Yet it was John Harrison, a self-educated carpenter by trade, who ultimately produced a series of clocks that proved extremely reliable—the H-1 (Harrison No. 1), H-2, and H-3. Britain's Board of Longitude officially recognized the achievement of Harrison for the H-1 in 1737. Ever the perfectionist, it was not until 1759, however, that he received enduring recognition for the H-4. Primary among its advances was size: the original H-1 had clocked in at seventy-five pounds, whereas the H-4 weighed only three.[9] This innovation combined with acclaim from Captain James Cook, who used a version during his ventures in the Pacific, favored mechanical timekeeping as a navigational strategy over stiff competition with lunar tables and the lunar distance method. Proponents of the latter technique, such as Harrison's archrival Nevil

Maskelyne, argued that with proper knowledge celestial navigation was available to all. What could be more trustworthy, celestial movements in the heavens or a unique, one-of-a-kind mechanical instrument invented by an eccentric autodidact?

The eccentric won. Consulting a watch, as anyone will tell you, is easier than mastering calendars of planetary motion—another death in the modern competition between machines versus natural know-how. Still, the adoption of mechanical timekeeping proved fateful. Not only did the clock help escalate imperial expansion during the nineteenth century through a new navigational confidence, but it abetted the increasing trust placed in the abilities of human-made machines over the natural world—an aspect we are too well acquainted with today. In the case of longitude, technology proved very useful. But the choice of the human over the celestial had enduring effects, to the point that there was no option after a while as political and business interests intruded. The heavens gradually receded. In this sense, the search for longitude is as important for understanding the rise of global capitalism as jet lag is for grasping the physiological limits of global capitalism in the present. Indeed, the measuring of longitude proved essential in the formal creation of time zones—the temporal infrastructure of jet lag. The world mapping of time emerged from this intersection of social and scientific endeavor during the late nineteenth century.

In 1884 the International Meridian Conference was held in Washington, DC, with the purpose of deciding a prime meridian for international timekeeping. The Greenwich Meridian was chosen as zero degrees longitude (0°), resulting in Greenwich Mean Time (GMT), though the use of Greenwich as a meridian went back to the founding of the observatory there. Coordinated Universal Time (UTC), a slight revision, succeeded GMT in 1960 and is still used today. Yet the establishment of universal standards reflected not only the continuing ascendance of scientific knowledge and precision about time, but also burgeoning business interests, like railroads and telegraph communications, that were concerned with synchronizing time schedules. "Railway time," whereby local time was coordinated with train timetables, had surfaced as a phenomenon during the 1840s, resulting in clocks at every station. Historian Vanessa Ogle has detailed how "time reform" became a social movement during the nineteenth century—in this case, with questions of standardization and "daylight saving" raised and promoted in parallel to social reform issues of child welfare and urban poverty.[10] These efforts at standardization faced resistance, however, at the local level, particularly across stretches of empire in Africa, the Middle East, and South Asia, where communities held fast to their own senses of time that were organized around religious calendars, lunar cycles, and other techniques of measurement—what On Barak has called "counter-tempos."[11] Such tensions did not merely reflect cultural differences, but palpable concerns for control over labor, leisure, and everyday life.

The point is that the implementation of universal standards of time faced social and political complexities, not simply scientific rivalries. Furthermore, the process of standardizing time differences remains incomplete. Despite its geographic immensity, China today has a single time zone. France uses Central European Time, even though it would be more accurate to use GMT since the prime meridian passes through France. Indian Standard Time is offset by thirty minutes (UTC +05:30) rather than adhering to an hourly demarcation. And a casual glance at time zones in the United States reveals the role of state boundaries in marking time. In this regard, the philosophical approaches to time discussed in the introduction must be complemented with this political gerrymandering of time—such perspectives and manipulations were not merely the product of high-minded thinkers with too much time on their hands. These eccentricities also underscore how heeding our bodies, not mechanical time, can prove more useful when coping with jet lag.

Indeed, while the scientific view of time as external to human perception continues to inform understandings of the universe, physicists like Henri Poincaré and Albert Einstein fundamentally revised Isaac Newton's seventeenth-century argument that time was absolute—"a single, constantly flowing river of time" as historian Peter Galison has written—by addressing problems of synchronizing time. As Galison argues, Poincaré deserves more credit than he has received for theories of time relativity, based on his work for the French *Bureau des Longitudes* and the difficulties he confronted, both practical and theoretical, in achieving synchronization. Put simply, two clocks—one in Paris and one in Berlin—may each say it is twelve noon, but this sense of simultaneity neglects the geographic distance between both places and, thus, the time it would take for a hypothetical signal traveling at the speed of light to make it from Paris to Berlin. This added time difference indicates there is no simultaneity. Fractions of a second matter. As such, time is dependent on spatial context. Space and time cannot be treated separately.[12]

Attentive to these elements plus gravity, Einstein's theory of relativity—first proposed in his article "On the Electrodynamics of Moving Bodies" (1905)—emerged from these practical considerations regarding time zones and global timekeeping. Einstein himself started out as a clerk in a patent office in Bern, Switzerland, after all. Attention to this cross-fertilization between the applied and the theoretical, the material and the abstract, points to the ineffective, if too common, dichotomy of "things *versus* thoughts," as Galison puts it, that has divided the history of science field, social history from intellectual history, and the disciplines of science, philosophy, and technology from one another.[13] In this sense, affinities should be drawn between such thinkers as Henri Bergson, Edmund Husserl, Poincaré, and Einstein with regard to time. Debates did exist. Einstein and Bergson publicly criticized one another—two Nobel Laureates representing not only their own contributions to time and relativity, but also embodying the broader competition between scientific and humanistic approaches to time.[14]

Such arguments highlight not simply the mutable nature of time or tensions between the "two cultures" of science and humanism, as C. P. Snow once described it. Rather, it points once more to an extensive backstory to jet lag that steps well beyond the exhaustion after getting off a plane. When we check our watches or phones and slowly adapt to a new time zone, we are consenting to a temporal world system that precedes us. When we negotiate the friction between how we physically feel and what time it is, we replay, however modestly, an intellectual drama about the nature and measurement of time. As with time itself, jet lag is not an illusion. But like time, its human-inflected elements leave us struggling to adapt, to perfect, and to transcend our existing limitations—against the immanence of nature.

Wrinkles in time

In her work *A Tenth of a Second* (2009), Jimena Canales describes how the modern period should not be defined exclusively by new ideologies and political revolutions—a grand narrative tradition—but should additionally be approached through scientific measurement.[15] The history of horology is a vital part of the history of modernity and its claims of progress. Yet the standardization of measurement has not been a straightforward process. In her case, the unit of a tenth of a second encountered wide debate in the fields of psychology, film, physics, and philosophy due to the belief that this fractional entity represented nothing less than the speed of thought. In a parallel vein, Thomas Pynchon has explored the imprecision, yet profound consequences, of scientific measurement in his historical novel *Mason & Dixon* (1997). Though early modern land surveying may not in itself be the most gripping theme imaginable, Pynchon uses it as an entry point for rewriting North American history. His true-life protagonists—the astronomer Charles Mason and the surveyor Jeremiah Dixon—were responsible for mapping the infamous border between Pennsylvania and Maryland just prior to the American Revolution, effectively creating the North-South divide that structured, if not caused, the American Civil War. What could be more appropriate than fiction to explore the fiction of territorial boundaries? The tragic undertone that builds in Pynchon's narrative is not only one of imminent war, but how human ambition can misappropriate scientific measurement and, ultimately, ruin knowledge. The astronomical occasion of the Transit of Venus early in the novel and the eventual surveying of the infamous line underscore this contrast between the celestial perfection of nature and the earthly folly of humankind.

Chris Marker raised similar questions of place, time, and fabrication, albeit in a more elusive, discursive fashion, in his essay-film *Sans Soleil* (1983). It is not about jet lag per se, but it nonetheless conveys a jet-lagged sensibility, given its concern for time and the narrative's longitudinal movements from Japan, to Guinea-Bissau, to San Francisco, and to Iceland. "He said that in the nineteenth century, mankind had come to terms with space. And that the great question of the twentieth was the coexistence of different concepts of time," a voice-over intones near the start of the film. This opening moment captures Marker's themes of kinesis and time, akin to *La Jetée*, but it also suggests a political orientation. His politics are best seen in his documentary on revolutionary Third Worldism, *A Grin Without a Cat* (1977). In this instance, however, his remark closely echoes a Marxist adage regarding the conquest of space and time by global capitalism. As Marx wrote in *Grundrisse* (1857–58), capitalism defies geographic boundaries in search of new markets with ever-faster speed and efficiency, resulting in "the annihilation of space by time."[16]

This perspective from the nineteenth century appears all too true today. Jet lag, it might be said, is what this

FIGURE 2.2 *Sans Soleil* (1983), directed by Chris Marker.

annihilation feels like. And yet it is incomplete. The method of annihilation that Marx speaks of—the speed of capitalism—seeks a simultaneity of production and consumption that is impossible to attain. Such speed remains subject to human limitations. Indeed, as the anthropologist Johannes Fabian has noted in a different setting, coevalness—that is, the mutual habitation of the same epochal time frame—has frequently been denied for contentious political and cultural reasons.[17] Under these particular circumstances, this may not be a bad thing. Walter Benjamin wrote about the "homogenous, empty time" of modernity, a notion that signaled the secularization of time and its expansive possibilities, but also the dread and uncertainty that could result, which demanded constant reconsideration of how to define progress.[18] By the same stroke, the dream of universal time—Babel's clock—that emerged from the seventeenth-century deliberations of Galileo and Newton requires a critical vigilance as to its uses and value—whether for scientific progress or the progress of capital. The concurrent emergence of modern time measurement and global capitalism is not coincidental. "The more we examine time, the more we identify it with a *character* we suspect and would like to unmask. And whose power and fascination we finally surrender to," E. M. Cioran has written. "From here to idolatry and bondage is only a step."[19]

3 CIRCADIAN RHYTHM AND BLUES

I sleep and unsleep.

—FERNANDO PESSOA,
***THE BOOK OF DISQUIET* (1982)**

It is curious to note the way in which we characterize personality types in relation to sleep. For example, we call people who work at night "night owls" and those who prefer the morning hours "morning larks" or "early birds." There is a direct association between time and bird life in this folk psychology. It is tempting, under the circumstances of this book, to say time and flight. Till Roenneberg, a professor of medical psychology and the author of *Internal Time* (2012), a book that examines the science of sleep, has discussed how these kinds of cultural proverbs are widespread, with early risers viewed as having advantage over late risers—even retaining a higher moral standing, with the latter often seen as lazy. Roenneberg resists this judgment, however. These cultural stereotypes precede the modern period, reflecting the fundamental importance of daylight in preindustrial societies for hunting, gathering, and similar life-sustaining activities.[1] But these popular characterizations do not explain why some people consistently wake early and some consistently late in the present.

William Gibson begins *Pattern Recognition* (2003)—unlike much of his work, a novel about the global present—by posing a provisional theory of jet lag during the introductory scene with his main protagonist, Cayce Pollard. As Gibson writes, after a long flight from London to New York, "Her mortal soul is leagues behind her, being reeled in on some ghostly umbilical down the vanished wake of the plane that brought her here, hundreds of thousands of feet above the Atlantic." "Souls can't move that quickly," Gibson continues, "and are left behind, and must be awaited, upon arrival, like lost luggage."[2] This passage strikingly resembles a moment in Bruce Chatwin's study of Aboriginal culture, *The Songlines* (1987). "A white explorer in Africa, anxious to press ahead with his journey, paid his porters for a series of forced marches. But they, almost within reach of their destination, set down their bundles and refused to budge," Chatwin describes. "No amount of extra payment would convince them otherwise. They said they had to wait for their souls to catch up."[3]

These interrelated moments from Roenneberg, Gibson, and Chatwin outline the parameters and focus of this chapter—the biology of sleep, cultures of motion and rest, and how they inform jet lag. Jet lag is typically comprised of restless nights, exhausted days, weakened mental aptitude, and other ailments, like loss of appetite and irritability, due to swift passage across time zones. We feel a sense of dislocation and loss, requiring time to catch up with ourselves. Indeed, proximate to Gibson and Chatwin's protagonists, this ephemeral state should force us to ponder the ways in which we relate to mechanical time versus biological time, privileging the former over the latter to our detriment. The preceding two chapters addressed two essential components of jet lag—aviation technology and the invisible infrastructure of global timekeeping we inhabit. Yet it is our human biology and "circadian" rhythms—from the Latin *circa* (around) and *diēm* (day)—regulated by the brain's hypothalamus that maintain our biological clocks, calibrating how we respond to speed and low-grade time travel. As captured by Gibson and Chatwin, the feelings of disorientation that travel can impart are not random or entirely individual but social and often connected to something deeper, whether we call it a soul or a physiological condition. Still, we increasingly ignore such internal timekeeping. Not only is time subject to manipulation to create different temporalities—what Johannes Fabian has termed the "schizogenic" use of time—but, more mundanely, time can be consciously or unconsciously ignored.[4] The French sociologist Georges Gurvitch categorized this occasion of temporal denial as "deceptive time" in his study *The Spectrum of Social Time* (1964), during which budding crises are momentarily concealed. This is a period of paradox and illusion, both benign and full of tension.[5]

Though Gurvitch worked on a societal scale, his argument can be seen in more ordinary ways, including narratives of jet lag. Noah Baumbach's film *Frances Ha* (2012) stars Greta Gerwig as Frances, a late twenty-something making her way in New York and finding herself caught between her college years and a more independent adulthood. Amid this limbo, Frances ignores certain time-related aspects of her life. More night owl than morning lark, her inability to attain her dream of being a professional dancer, to let go of her college best friend, and to achieve a general sense of autonomy lead her through a series of setbacks prompted by money, her own ill-thought decisions, and the decisions of others. After her closest friend Sophie (Mickey Sumner) leaves their living situation to pursue a relationship, Frances lives briefly with two male acquaintances in Chinatown, returns home for Christmas in Sacramento, and eventually hits bottom by working a summer session at her alma mater in order to accrue some savings—a moment of regression that enables her to turn a corner. Before this experience, she makes an impromptu trip to Paris for a weekend, a poor choice given her finances, but based on an offer of free lodging. Despite the promise of a Parisian escape, Frances is slammed by jet lag, unable to sleep and then asleep until late afternoon her first day there. She never hears from a friend. She reads Proust. The cycle repeats itself the next day. She soon finds herself returning to New York, unfulfilled.

This episode is another mistake in a prolonged list for Frances, but it neatly summarizes how we fail to anticipate

FIGURE 3.1 *Frances Ha* (2012), directed by Noah Baumbach.

jet lag. We prefer to deceive ourselves. Jet lag comes second
to the imagined freedom of travel. Unlike Charlotte in *Lost
in Translation* for whom jet lag opens up a set of possibilities
and life rumination, Frances bears the brunt of jet lag as most
of us do—a discomfort to endure, the beginning and end of
its passage unclear. Frances experiences the Platonic ideal of
jet lag. Yet Baumbach's depiction, with the small, wry tie-in of
In Search of Lost Time, amplifies a common flaw that Frances
possesses, which many of us possess. She is not simply bad
with money (as many of us are), but she is bad with time (as
many of us are). Her spontaneity costs her both ways. This
realization pushes her to resolve her financial woes through
the summer job upstate and her time issues about where
she stands in life. Baumbach, like Coppola, uses jet lag as
a temporal idiom to approach and think about maturity—

confronting time by confronting time. Or, what some have called, emotional jet lag.[6]

But biology matters, too. Confronting time also means confronting physiology.

Darkness at noon

"I know one thing. When I sleep, I know no fear, no trouble, no bliss. Blessing on him who invented sleep. The common coin that purchases all things, the balance that levels shepherd and king, fool and wise man," reads Kris Kelvin (Donatas Banionis), the main character in Andrei Tarkovsky's cerebral science-fiction film *Solaris* (1972). "There is only one bad thing about sound sleep. They say it closely resembles death." *Solaris* is based on a 1961 novel by Stanislaw Lem, about a psychologist who visits a remote space station. Astronauts there have suffered hallucinations and other strange phenomena related to the planet Solaris, which the station is orbiting. However, these lines originate from *Don Quixote*—a jarring, but deliberate, juxtaposition by Tarkovsky that enhances the chronological and intellectual depth of the film.[7] Indeed, this citation speaks to the film's enquiries regarding reality and the aesthetic of realism: the film can be viewed as a tacit critique of Stalinist socialist realism. As part of their mutual interrogation of reality, both Tarkovsky and Cervantes address the role and purpose of sleep—its universality, its palliative qualities, yet also

FIGURE 3.2 *Solaris* (1972), directed by Andrei Tarkovsky.

its virtual lifelessness, approaching death. It is a condition between physical and dream worlds, its reveries favoring an emotional truth over a material one. Even so, a bias toward wakefulness—as implied, with an ironic touch, in the opening epigraph by Fernando Pessoa—defines our lives. What is sleep? And why must we experience it?

As with many such questions in this book, a wide spectrum of ongoing research has been established, looking at disorders ranging from insomnia to excessive sleepiness, with conditions such as narcolepsy, sleep apnea, and restless legs syndrome (Willis-Ekbom disease) in between these extremes. By the same stroke, existing answers have their roots in antiquity. The nature of sleep preoccupied Plato. He believed it was an intermediate state between being and non-being. His student Aristotle similarly considered sleep "a border-land between living and not-living: a person who is asleep would appear to be neither completely non-existent nor completely existent—for of course it is to the waking state *par excellence* that life pertains."[8] He further pondered the need for sleep in his short treatise *On Sleep and Sleeplessness* (c. 350 BC), concluding it renewed the senses and was managed by the stomach.

What we call sleep hygiene today has been of long-standing importance for different religious faiths—determined by morning and evening prayers, for example. Dreams have played a significant role in Greco-Roman, Judeo-Christian, Buddhist, Hindu, Native American, and African religious traditions as an idiom for receiving otherworldly messages. The fourteenth-century Islamic scholar Ibn Khaldūn drafted a taxonomy of three kinds of dreams: those from Allah, those from angels, and those from Satan. Rather than comprising a state of complete non-being, sleep and dreaming instead permitted another way of being in the world, a contrast not only from Plato and Aristotle, but also from many philosophical views in the modern Western tradition discussed earlier.

This tradition has nonetheless influenced how sleep is understood today. René Descartes, the seventeenth-century thinker considered to be the founder of modern philosophy, countered Aristotle's belief that sleep was ruled by the stomach to argue that the brain was more important, specifically the pineal gland where he thought the soul resided. The pineal gland is in fact where melatonin, a key hormone in the regulation of sleep and circadian rhythms, is produced. More vital than Descartes, however, during this period was the eighteenth-century astronomer Jean-Jacques d'Ortous de Mairan and his unlikely work on plant biology.

In the summer of 1729, de Mairan noticed how a potted mimosa would furl and unfurl its leaves on a daily basis corresponding to nighttime and daytime, thus raising a profound question. Did plants "sleep" in the same way as humans and animals? De Mairan not only conjectured this proposition to be true, but he conducted a set of experiments involving the placement of his plant in darkness, which startlingly indicated that the mimosa's cycle of furling and unfurling did not necessarily depend on the presence of light. The plant appeared to possess instead an internal mechanism that followed cycles of day and night, though without external stimuli—a wonder of natural timekeeping later echoed in Paul Klee's characteristically playful work *Uhrpflanzen (Clock-Plants)* from 1924.

These observations by de Mairan presaged the scientific field of chronobiology today. Every living organism—plant or animal, blue whale or micro-bacterium—has an internal biological clock. Chronobiology, as the name suggests, is the study of how these living clocks work and how this timekeeping not only affects daily matters of sleeping and alertness, but also longer-term cycles of aging and biological decline. As the contingencies of history would have it, the field of chronobiology was first contemplated as a separate discipline during the mid-1960s—the same period as jet lag's first diagnosis. A scientific meeting in Germany held under the rubric "Circadian Clocks" explored this proposal, though chronobiology was not officially recognized as an independent discipline until 1979.[9] It had gradually emerged

FIGURE 3.3 Paul Klee, *Uhrpflanzen (Clock-Plants)* (1924).

from different fields such as botany, zoology, and medicine, which left unclear the usefulness of a more integrated, autonomous discipline—and a long way from putting potted plants in and out of cupboards. Yet this longevity for chronobiology to be established tells a story. De Mairan's early modern experiments did not attract immediate or enduring attention.

His insights required the rise of modern industrialization, its mechanical time, and its human exhaustion for scientists to take deeper notice.

It should be stressed that chronobiology is not exclusively concerned with sleep or modern human fatigue. But neither has this subject been insulated from real-world applications. In his book *24/7* (2013), the critic Jonathan Crary has noted how the US Defense Department has committed substantial resources to studying the white-crowned sparrow—a migratory bird that is able to stay awake for up to seven days during its seasonal migrations between Mexico and Alaska. The assumption is that the science behind this avian ability could contribute to developing "sleep-resistant" soldiers that could undertake "missions of indefinite duration"—one step toward sleepless workers and sleepless consumers, Crary surmises, given frequent leaps of innovation from military to private sector use.[10]

Such research is not new. The first sleep laboratory was founded in 1925 at the University of Chicago by the physiologist Nathaniel Kleitman, who, in 1938, spent thirty-two days in Mammoth Cave in Kentucky in order to study the effects of the absence of sunlight on sleep patterns. He discovered that the human body maintained a roughly twenty-four-hour cycle of temperature fluctuation that regulated sleep and wakefulness, indicating an internal, or endogenous, clock. Kleitman went on to publish *Sleep and Wakefulness* (1939), a classic in the field that introduced the concept of a "basic rest-activity cycle" (BRAC) to describe how the body controlled fatigue and alertness for cycles between one to two hours. With his student Eugene Aserinsky, he later detected "rapid eye movement" (REM), a period of heightened brain activity while sleeping that contributed to dreaming. For these reasons, Kleitman has been deemed the father of sleep research.

Though a long intercontinental flight can also resemble waiting it out in a cave, this foundation of research has nonetheless proved widely influential. Franz Halberg, a medical doctor at the University of Minnesota, devised the term "circadian" during the 1950s. The botanist Erwin Bünning, the biologist Jürgen Aschoff, and the biologist Colin Pittendrigh expanded research beyond human health to other organisms, plants and animals alike, and are considered the founders of the broader discipline of chronobiology as a result. These combined efforts help us understand jet lag today. Aschoff, for example, replicated Kleitman's earlier Mammoth Cave experiment by constructing an underground bunker near Andechs in Bavaria to examine concurrent biological rhythms as well as the potential for internal de-synchronization—that is, modifying a person's biological clock.[11] This research during the late 1960s not only confirmed the continued functioning of internal clocks in environments of sensory isolation. It also reinforced the complexity of interaction between external factors, such as shifting patterns of light, and inherited evolutionary features that stabilized bodily timekeeping, by sustaining a twenty-four-hour cycle through a variety of conditions. Indeed, the recurrent absence of perfect harmony between changing environmental circumstances and endogenous rhythms revealed not the faultiness of evolution, but the exact opposite: the body's ability to adjust daily, seasonally, and geographically without a person's health going into rapid decline as a consequence of a genetically fixed physiological routine. Our bodies may appear to be imperfect clocks—too individual and thus ill-suited to the rigid schedules of modern life. But they are, in fact, more responsive and adaptable to life's contingencies than the mechanical instruments of timekeeping we abide by.

Technology can precipitously unsettle this equilibrium of stability and adaptation. Jet lag is a prime example of artificially induced de-synchronization, but it is not a solitary one. Long hours operating machinery, patrolling city streets at night, working the graveyard shift at a fluorescent-lit hospital, or sitting at a desk looking at an unchanging, brightly illuminated screen—all can disrupt our biological rhythms if we do not listen to what our bodies tell us. As referred to earlier, our techno-crepuscular malaise—an inability to escape the intrusion of unnatural light through hand held devices and similar technology—is becoming increasingly omnipresent. Nighttime has been diminished; we live in a perpetual, artificial twilight.

Specific to air travel, the speed of aviation impairs our body's ability to respond quickly and without notice, unlike daily or seasonal changes to labor and life routine. The problem of speed is what makes us not just tired, but exhausted at unusual times—a feeling of darkness at

FIGURE 3.4 "Ninety Years without Slumbering" (1963), *The Twilight Zone*, directed by Roger Kay.

noon, to misappropriate Arthur Koestler. This arrhythmic weariness highlights the specific "chronotypes" (internal time settings) that define us individually. To return to the topoi of night owls and morning larks, this distinction is not entirely a product of social learning, but is hardwired into our genes. Human beings are not universally synchronized, to the despair of classroom attendance takers the world over. While age can affect sleep, with babies, children, and youth typically needing more sleep than adults, this genetic predisposition cannot be changed. The periodic dissonance between our innate timekeeping and the disruptive patterns of modern life constitute, what Till Roenneberg has called, social jet lag.

The upshot is that sleep and the disturbance of sleep cycles, as with classic jet lag, are not easily corrected. They necessitate patience for the body's timekeeping to recalibrate itself, like any clock. Yet too often we unduly fix our well-being to the logic and demands of mechanical time, rather than a more natural time, akin to the character of Sam Forstmann (Ed Wynn) in *The Twilight Zone* episode "Ninety Years without Slumbering" (1963). An allegory of aging and obedience to automated time, Forstmann believes he will die if the grandfather clock he maintains was to stop working. When it does stop, he does not feel a mortal blow, but liberation from a purely imagined bondage.

Remain in light

"Speed, it seems to me, provides the one genuinely modern pleasure," Aldous Huxley wrote in his essay "Wanted, a New Pleasure" (1931). "True, men have always enjoyed speed; but their enjoyment has been limited, until very recent times, by the capacities of the horse, whose maximum velocity is not much more than thirty miles per hour," he explained, echoing Italo Calvino as cited earlier. "Now thirty miles an hour on a horse feels very much faster than sixty miles an hour in a train or a hundred in an airplane. The train is too large and steady, the airplane too remote from stationary surroundings, to give their passengers a very intense sensation of speed. The automobile is sufficiently small and sufficiently near the ground to be able to compete, as an intoxicating speed-purveyor, with the galloping horse."[12] Enda Duffy, whose book *The Speed Handbook* (2009) includes this passage, has taken Huxley's perspective as a starting point for an aesthetics of speed and modernity. Speed gave motion and *feeling* to being modern. Huxley was not alone.

"We affirm that the world's magnificence has been enriched by a new beauty: the beauty of speed," Filippo Tommaso Marinetti celebrated in the *Manifesto of Futurism* (1909). As promoted by the Italian Futurist movement, which worshiped speed as an ideal, the politics of speed during the early twentieth century blended newfound elements of technological access, popular consumption, and personal power. Speed was understood in both literal and abstract terms. Unlike Huxley and his stress on the car, the Italian *Aeropittura* ("Aeropainting") group believed the airplane provided a new aesthetic vantage point that must be seized, countering a terrestrial bias that had long inhabited art history, as outlined in the *Manifesto of Aeropainting* (1929).[13] Tullio Crali and his painting *Nose-Diving on the City* (1939), the best-known artist and work from this circle today, captures this aerial perspective, the supremacy of machines, and the vertiginous feeling of modern velocity that could be achieved. However, this kind of supremacy translated into a disastrous politics, with many Italian futurists, including Marinetti, embracing fascism, in the misguided belief that it, too, provided a speedy departure from the past into a sublime future.

These ideas touch upon a recurrent theme. If one method of being modern is to be intensely aware of time, speed is a technique for this awareness, for grasping time, calculated through distance divided by time. Jet lag instantiates this space-time intersection. Yet speed can still be elusive, an element beyond measurement. As Duffy describes, the *sensation* of speed is crucial. After a preceding age of modern

FIGURE 3.5 Tullio Crali, *Incuneandosi nell'abitato (Nose-Diving on the City)* (1939).

exploration, it provided "a means to experience space in a new way, at the very moment when there was no more new world space left to organize."[14] Indeed, as noted by Huxley, this sensation is more acutely felt when physically close to the ground, as in an automobile or on a horse—a point elaborated by Roland Barthes in his short piece "The Jet-Man" from *Mythologies* (1957). Barthes writes that the enigma of the jet age is how speed through modern aviation became internalized—a source of physical ambiguity, rather than an enhanced thrill through acceleration. In contrast to the "pilot-hero" prior to the jet age, the paradox of the jet-man is that he experiences the vitality of motionlessness, of "going faster than speed," and thus feeling something entirely new and different. In Barthes's words, "Motion is no longer the optical perception of points and surfaces; it has become a kind of vertical disorder, made of contractions, black-outs, terrors and faints; it is no longer a gliding but an inner devastation, an unnatural perturbation, a motionless crisis of bodily consciousness."[15]

What Barthes describes is what we would call jet lag today. Though his immediate critical concern was to demythologize the modern pilot as hero, these passing thoughts on the "coenaesthesis" of jet travel underscored the contradictory effects of modern technological innovation—at once improving and worsening human life through state-of-the-art acceleration. I said before that jet lag is a collateral effect of global capitalism: jet lag is what globalization feels like. Barthes's prescient commentary strengthens this claim by emphasizing how acceleration is not always visible to the naked eye—a matter of "optical perception of points and surfaces" as he puts it—but instead an internal condition centered on physiological response, not conscious reflection. Being modern can be about how one feels, rather than how one looks, about what is hidden and invisible, rather than what is outward spectacle.

Yet such physical reactions are often observable, as Martin Amis has nakedly depicted in his apropos novel *Money* (1984). "I am a thing made up of time lag, culture shock, zone shift. Human beings simply weren't meant to fly around like this," Amis comments in the voice of his passenger anti-hero, John Self. "Scorched throat, pimpled vision, memory wipes—nothing new to me, but it's all much worse these days, now that I ride the planet shuttle. I have to get up in the middle of the night to check out the can. My daily tiredness peak arrives exactly when it wants to, often after morning coffee. . . . All day I am my night self, spliced by night thoughts, night sweats. And all night, well, I am something else entirely, something else again, I am something overevolved, a salty slipstream thinning out and trailing down over the black Atlantic."[16]

This passage foreshadows Gibson's later trans-Atlantic episode. Speed incapacitates their twin protagonists, in closely related language. Nonetheless, contra John Self, the best treatment for jet lag, as recommended by the National Sleep Foundation, is to avoid stimulants, to stay awake until evening at one's point of arrival, and to remain in sunlight (as much as possible), to revise the title of a Talking Heads album. These methods allow for one's body to adjust as swiftly as possible to the natural time conditions of a new locale. A person's internal clock needs to recalibrate, which can take days—on average a day for each hour gained or lost. Jet lag from flying west to east can be more difficult for this reason, since traveling ahead in time can mean a shorter day upon arrival and, thus, fewer hours of daylight to adapt.[17] But these factors are variable, depending on the length of one's flight and the arrival time. Intercontinental flights are usually scheduled to land in the morning for this reason. Varying one's diet has also been prescribed. The Argonne Anti-Jet-Lag diet alternates feasting and fasting, four days before flying, in order to prep the body for a time change. The rationale is that biological rhythms are not only attuned to light cycles, but also dietary routines.[18] A more recent technique has been light therapy, which uses exposure to flashing lights to modify a person's internal clock gradually before and after travel.[19]

The important point is that our biological clocks matter. They do not adjust quickly. There is no permanent cure for jet lag, only treatment. But many of these recommendations fall into a broader category of sleep hygiene: practices for improving the quality of sleep through diet, routine, and supervising technology use prior to sleep. Our technological ambitions and the progressive acceleration of modern life continue to exceed our biological abilities—a situation of limits, not unlike those of Icarus.

Call it sleep

As cited in the introduction, jet lag was first identified during the mid-1960s. An article in the *Los Angeles Times* from February 13, 1966, is reported to be the first to use the expression, a riff on the cultural notion of a "jet set."[20] Jet lag has subsequently reflected this combination of science and humanism, as underscored throughout this book. But what has come to be called "jet lag" was noticed earlier, as Barthes's remarks indicate. The US Federal Aviation Agency (today's FAA) issued a report in March 1965 entitled "Pilot Fatigue: Intercontinental Jet Flight" about a series of tests conducted during two flights from Oklahoma City to Tokyo and back, since "the disruption of physiological day-night cycling" had been observed as "a consequence of rapid translocation through many time zones." In the wording of the report, flight-produced "time lag" raised questions about its effect in generating a "biological lag time" resulting in "an undesirable level of both acute and chronic fatigue."[21]

This pilot study, so to speak, was not unusual. Interest in the medical impact of flight had existed since the nineteenth century. The French physiologist Paul Bert is considered the father of aviation medicine for his work on the health effects of air pressure and oxygen. Subsequent researchers and physicians—for instance Louis H. Bauer, who wrote *Aviation Medicine* (1926) and founded the Aerospace Medical Association in 1929—addressed the influence of flying on fitness through varying conditions of speed, altitude, and hypoxia. Publications like *Aerospace Medicine and Human Performance*, *Chronobiology International*, and the *Journal of Circadian Rhythms* testify to the continuing growth and expansion of medical and scientific research with concern not solely for jet lag, but for rest, sleep, and modern fatigue more generally.

Yet zombies—that unavoidable pop zeitgeist—may tell us more about the contemporary cultural meanings of exhaustion than these academic journals combined. Monsters are expressions of social anxiety. Mary Shelley's *Frankenstein* (1818) depicted apprehensions about modern science, while Bram Stoker's *Dracula* (1897) regards the life-sucking nature of industrial capitalism, according to critic Franco Moretti.[22] Zombies once implied racial fear, especially during the early twentieth century, with their purported association with African "voodoo" as seen in *White Zombie* (1932). Zombies in film have since represented angst over disease—

FIGURE 3.6 *World War Z* (2013), directed by Marc Forster.

as in *Resident Evil* (2002), *28 Days Later* (2002), and their assorted sequels—as well as distress about overpopulation, government response, and bureaucratic coordination, a set of interrelated themes found in *World War Z* (2013).

Zombies have also long been associated with labor, going back to plantation slavery in the Caribbean. The myth of zombies first emerged among African men and women, who at times appeared neither dead nor among the living due to the physical brutality of slavery. In her oft-neglected ethnographic work, Zora Neale Hurston once described zombies as "bodies without souls."[23] In like fashion, zombies today have come to signify the exhausted nature of present-day life. The demanding pace of global capitalism has rendered many neither living nor not-living, to paraphrase Aristotle. The TV show *The Walking Dead* (2010-present) has insinuated this view, with its zombie "walkers" denoting not only an immediate mortal threat, but also a menacing context for human "survivors" to navigate social relationships that prove less predictable. The premise of the show resembles many corporate settings, ones populated by fraught teams surrounded by anonymous threats that will never allow rest, day or night. Zombies are ultimately human after all.

Sleep is precious. It is even being monetized. We sleep not for the sake of rest, but to be better workers. One imagines Aldous Huxley's notion of "sleep-learning" (hypnopedia) described in *Brave New World* (1932) becoming a reality, as another means of utilizing sleep. And yet this basic human necessity is being increasingly undervalued, too. The German philosopher Reinhart Koselleck once argued that a "peculiar form of acceleration" has defined modernity.[24] This unabated pace—a speed without ecstasy—is generating detrimental consequences, of which jet lag is only one example. In the same way that we have lost track of popular understandings about planetary movements since the nineteenth century—the celestial importance of the nighttime—so too are we failing to accommodate recuperative rest in our hurrisome lives. We lack a philosophy of sleep that restores balance and value to day and night.

Latitude, which tracks annual cycles of seasonal light and darkness, and longitude, which measures the daily east-to-west movement of the sun across the sky, both remain significant for pinpointing time and location. Once revealing both problems and solutions to standardizing time, they help explain jet lag. But they are also vital coordinates for the potential of sleep—if we allow ourselves to listen to our own bodies and observe the natural rhythms of the world, instead of the illusory dictates of mechanical timekeeping.

4 HEAVEN UP HERE

*You've got nothing to fear/It may be hell down there/
Cause it's Heaven up here.*

**— ECHO AND THE BUNNYMEN,
"HEAVEN UP HERE" (1981)**

Aircraft convey a modern glamour. Arrival shots of states-
men, musicians, and other celebrities stepping onto an airport tarmac enhance the power of those involved, with the
capacity of flight transferring an aura of authority, regardless
of any jet lag present. This kind of red carpet treatment—a
tarmac politics—serves as a terrestrial coda to the luxury one
imagines onboard: personal service, domestic furnishing,
and privacy undisturbed by other passengers. For those
of us who travel commercial, the aura of landing is less so,
our experiences being faint facsimiles of an older, grander,
more authentic form of arrival, as Walter Benjamin might
put it, when flying was unique. To return to an observation
made earlier, this loss of enchantment can be attributed to
the ordinariness of flight today and the diminishment of its

primal romance. In his bestselling *Future Shock* (1970), Alvin Toffler referred to this relationship between the familiar and the unfamiliar as the "novelty ratio"—in this instance, the non-routine of flight has become routine.[1] And yet there are still enclaves of pleasure to be found.

"Nowhere was the airport's charm more concentrated than on the screens placed at intervals across the terminal which announced, in deliberately workmanlike fonts, the itineraries of aircraft about to take to the skies. These screens implied a feeling of infinite and immediate possibility," Alain de Botton writes in his account of being the first writer-in-residence at London's Heathrow International Airport. "The lack of detail about the destinations served only to stir unfocused images of nostalgia and longing: Tel Aviv, Tripoli, St. Petersburg, Miami, Muscat via Abu Dhabi, Algiers, Grand Cayman via Nassau . . . all of these promises of alternative lives, to which we might appeal at moments of claustrophobia and stagnation."[2] What de Botton touches upon here is the undiminished promise of travel—to escape our ordinary lives—as insinuated by departure timetables and the sheer physical structure of the airport itself. Travel is understood in both senses of the term *flight*, whether from home, country, seasonal climate, or frenetic culture. We seek to go somewhere *different*. Yet the actual experience of travel can fall well short of this mark, our desires for an alternative life, however temporary, remaining unfulfilled—another kind of cruel optimism.

FIGURE 4.1 Charles de Gaulle Airport, July 2016.

Jet lag can be a contributing factor to this disappointment—our physical bodies unable to catch up in efficient time to wherever our imaginations lead us. But modern travel possesses other lags, social and cultural, as well. Similar to the characters of Charlotte in *Lost in Translation* and Frances in *Frances Ha*, we can encounter in stark relief the very issues we seek to avoid, whether personal or societal in scope. This chapter regards this paradox. It is about the culture of travel and how jet lag is both a condition of this milieu as well as a metaphorical means for interpreting it. As addressed before, jet lag is an effect of technological innovation, the global mapping of time, and our own biorhythms. It is also the outcome of travel—a patently obvious point and yet, as a result, one treated in passing, without considered deliberation. We reminisce of home and humblebrag about our adventures elsewhere, but we grumble and complain, if we speak at all, about the time and process of travel itself. Like jet lag, we do not dwell enough on this aspect and what it tells us about living with, and through, contemporary globalization.

What is subsequently proposed in this memo-non-lecture is that travel does not offer escapism or a subterfuge from our everyday existence, but precisely the opposite: it can heighten our sense of reality. In the same way that jet lag, when mindfully measured, can reveal the malignant repercussions of technological innovation on our bodies, the experience of being a passenger can reinforce social hierarchies instead of departing from them. Gender norms, racial differences, class politics, and other matters of society that we think we have left behind at the terminal still reside within whatever cabin we find ourselves. At times this fact of public anxieties spilling over into the experience of flight is painfully clear, as with numerous onboard episodes of religious profiling since 9/11. Unable to exit, we are captive to such incidents, held hostage by our fears—a predicament implicitly captured with B-movie élan in *Snakes on a Plane* (2006). Onboard cabins can be microcosms of social conflict. Despite the potential freedom of being away from social norms and above the law where terrestrial rules do not apply, whether through duty-free shopping or sexual promiscuity (a.k.a. the "mile high" club), the culture of flight frequently exhibits its own kind of time lag—a postponement of social progress, regardless of the modern gloss of the aircraft itself.

FIGURE 4.2 *Snakes on a Plane* (2006), directed by David R. Ellis.

Society of the airport

I have been deported exactly once in my life, during the writing of this book as chance would have it. I failed to have two blank pages in my passport, a requirement for entrance into South Africa. Despite having traveled there for over two decades without incident, I could not get through passport control at Oliver Tambo International Airport in Johannesburg as a result of this new rule administered by the South African Department of Home Affairs. It had happened to others, I was reassured. Yet it was a moment of frustration, of physical exhaustion, of utter emotional depletion. I had to cancel plans I had made months in advance, and, moreover, I had departed from Austin and would require making that particular journey back again, approximately twenty-four hours of travel time. One stroke of good fortune was that I gained entrance to the Lufthansa business lounge, where I could wait before my return flight. Unlike so many refugees and asylum seekers, my experience was minor. Nonetheless, resigned to my fate of temporary statelessness, day and night soon blurred. Jet lag took over. My organized sense of celestial motion outside the terminal became unclear, the sky imparting a mysterious half-light akin to Giorgio de Chirico's *The Enigma of a Day* (1914) or René Magritte's *The Empire of Light* (c. 1954). Mechanical time became meaningless, too. I was only concerned about the hour of my return flight to Washington Dulles, and the total number of hours required before I would be back home in Texas. I took a shower and foraged from the hot bar. I sent email and tried to read. Normality eluded me. Jet lag had become a provisional state of social being.

Contra many prevailing opinions, the anthropologist James Clifford has written that travel encompasses "an increasingly complex range of experiences," representing "practices of crossing and interaction" that in turn complicate "the localism of many common assumptions about culture."[3] Travel, in his view, has been construed as the anti-thesis of culture—the latter word originating from the Latin root word for cultivating, gardening, and establishing a permanent home. As he writes, "dwelling" has been understood as a primary practice of civic life, with travel being a "supplement" to this principle mode of living. However, he resists this discrete perspective, preferring the interplay between dwelling and traveling and the varying roles of immigration, expulsion, and exile in the constitution of culture. The title

FIGURE 4.3 Giorgio de Chirico, *The Enigma of a Day* (1914).

of his book *Routes* underscores this dynamic relationship, being a phonetic double entendre. Rather than traveling between cultures, travel *is* a form of culture. Clifford's approach falls into a deeper intellectual tradition mentioned before, including such philosopher-wanderers as Thoreau, Nietzsche, and Baudelaire and protagonists of fiction like Odysseus, Kurtz, and Huckleberry Finn, who gained self-realization through travel. The recent popularity of such writers and intellectuals as Elizabeth Gilbert, Cheryl Strayed, and Rebecca Solnit points to a gendered absence and vital correction to this literary custom. As George Santayana wrote in his essay "The Philosophy of Travel," movement is "the privilege of animals," enabling human intelligence itself.[4]

The airport would appear to be an empowering element for such travel knowledge, and indeed it often is. The critic Alastair Gordon has written how early airport architecture raised provocative questions of function versus style, drawing upon railway stations and classical architecture as well as grasping its symbolic importance for setting "the stage for the adventure of flight."[5] Airports are sites of nostalgia, public and private, that can trigger forms of emotional jet lag.[6] And yet airports are increasingly about control and security, rather than freedom and imagination. Airports possess a paradox of choice and constraint, a tension between danger and safety. Terminals capture a queer confluence of the civic and the commercial, with border agents and retail sales associates commingling with passengers. They serve as spectacles of futurism and modernity, but they can also be malformed expressions of these ideas, undergirded by anxieties of disaster, whether due to technological imperfection or human agency.

In these ways, airports are not separate from society—liminal points between, what the French theorist Marc Augé has called, "the here and the elsewhere"—but instead are dense condensations of society.[7] As nodal spaces of cultural kinesis, airports are the intersectional ground of multiple trends—technological, economic, social, and political. Sarah Sharma has contended that airports reflect a global pattern of social homogenization and apolitical life, with "the retreat of individuals into their own personal technospheres" while waiting in departure lounges echoing "a larger withdrawal of citizens from activating public space."[8] On the other hand, they can serve as sites of political protest, as witnessed in demonstrations at airports across the United States following a travel ban on refugees and citizens of Iran, Iraq, Libya, Syria, Yemen, Somalia, and Sudan as ordered by US President Donald Trump. Paul Virilio has proposed that the airport is "the new city" catering to millions of people each year, increasingly more than older "spatial" cities defined by natural features of place. Airports are intersections of time and speed, highlighting their value. A bleak *habitus* of constantly arriving and departing, rather than settling and dwelling, has consequently taken hold. "People are no longer citizens," Virilio writes, "they're passengers in transit."[9]

If airports remain spaces of culture, they are unusual ones. Augé has designated airports as "non-places"—a term first used by Michel de Certeau to describe "spaces" of temporary habitation in contrast to "places" of residence. "The traveler's space may thus be the archetype of *non-place*," Augé asserts.[10] In this sense, the airport-as-non-place can be likened to jet lag-as-non-time: the former being a spatial analog to the latter's temporal condition. Both are transient. Yet both exhibit forms and effects of "supermodernity" where spectacle is the prevalent ethos.[11] Individuals in transit observe and *feel* the marvel of innovation, as with jet lag, but do not pause to analyze or critique.

The alluring wonder of this supermodernity can be witnessed by anyone who has walked through an international departure gate at a major airport—think London Heathrow, Hong Kong, or Dubai—where high-end stores have become the norm. Passengers in transit are subject to the global capitalist spectacle of Dolce & Gabbana, Giorgio Armani, Gucci, and other fashionable brands for clothing, watches, and single malt whiskey, among other items. Airports have been hybridized into shopping malls, replete with food courts and their obligatory McDonald's, Starbucks, and Panda Express franchises. Jet setting today rests in buying, not flying, with the excitement of travel driven by consumer tastes and terminal window-shopping. This situation is a variation of what Guy Debord once described as the "society of the spectacle" in which social relations are determined by images and representation. In his words, "The modern spectacle depicts what society *could* deliver, but in so doing it rigidly separates what is *possible* from what is *permitted*."[12] This separation as materialized in airport terminals can occur in terms of security—non-places can be spaces of extreme anxiety, with spectacles of terrorism and semi-sovereign police apparatuses—though also along more familiar social lines: race, class, and gender among them. Airports continue to convey fantasies of the future, but through consumption not aviation, capitalist self-fashioning not social progress. Airports present an infrastructure for anticipating and coping with the non-time of jet lag, whether through business lounges, spas,

FIGURE 4.4 Incheon International Airport, May 2016.

or vendors selling neck pillows. But they still perpetuate certain social lags of their own.

Leaving on a jet plane

If the romance of flying can be attributed to its mix of innovation, acceleration, and mortal danger, commercial travel has placed a premium on comfort. The dreams of passengers and pilots must not be confused. Vertigo, nausea, and exhaustion generated anxieties well before the jet age. Indeed, flight has always put us in touch with our physical well-being, with jet lag residing among an assortment of travel ailments. Such concerns have produced solutions that continue to be revised today, though without undermining revenue. The profitability of early passenger service depended on speed, particularly for transcontinental travel, given existing competition with railways. Providing two kinds of passage helped. Boeing Air Transport and National Air Transport were among the first to carry both mail and passengers in 1927, undertaking a route between San Francisco and New York. The experience of flying for these new passengers resembled the adventure it still was, with luggage carefully weighed and cotton balls and gum provided for the tremendous noise and sudden altitude shifts in an unpressurized cabin. These passengers flew along with the mail and were often a secondary concern. Conditions were primitive, with onboard accommodation similar to the pilot's—and at times worse. For several hundred dollars (one way), a passenger would have to wear a flight suit and parachute and withstand the fatigue of a 2,600-mile journey that lasted as long as thirty-two hours with as many as fifteen connections, in addition to sitting aside bundles of mail in a noise-filled aircraft. The feeling of romance could wear thin.

Traveling alongside stacks of postal mail gradually transitioned to an experience proximate to train travel in a furnished cabin, albeit with turbulence and weather exposure. An unpressurized cabin meant not only thinner levels of oxygen (not unlike mountaineering) and nausea from abrupt altitude changes, but it also entailed intense cold or heat depending on the season. The speed of propeller flight allowed for windows to be rolled down for fresh air. But queasiness from engine fumes also posed a constant problem. The toilet, if available, was often a cut out hole that opened into vertiginous airspace.

A solution to this minimalist situation and its assorted challenges was the hiring of nurses to attend to the comfort and needs of passengers midflight, starting in the 1930s. Though flight attendants were on board zeppelins, Ellen Church is regarded as the first flight stewardess as cited earlier, commencing this position on a flight for Boeing in May 1930. Other carriers soon followed. These flight stewardesses had been preceded by the intermittent use of "cabin boys," a practice started by Daimler Airway and Imperial Airways in Great Britain during the 1920s. Women had not been viewed as capable of handling the dangers of flight. Nevertheless, "sky girls" quickly became a feature of commercial aviation with multiple tasks involved, including ticketing, baggage handling, and fueling the plane, in addition to onboard hospitality. Pre-prepared food was also provided, and this early period became known as the "fried-chicken era," named after the most common meal served. Sandwiches and fruit were also on offer, as well as coffee and water out of Thermoses. But the unsteadiness of small planes at a low altitude could make meals an unappealing proposition. Smoking was allowed. Entertainment was otherwise nominal, with the experience of flying itself being the entertainment—a sublime view of the world from on high.

Women flight attendants popularized aviation, delivering a sense of domesticity to a demanding world defined by daily

FIGURE 4.5 Amelia Earhart (c. 1928).

risks of mechanical failure, bad weather, and inexperienced pilots. As symbolized by the gender-bending boldness of Amelia Earhart—with her iconic tomboy haircut, pants, and leather flight jacket (Earhart eventually had her own clothing line)—aviation promised new opportunities for redefining womanhood. Indeed, Earhart was not an anomaly but conformed to an interwar archetype of a new modern woman—the flapper, personifying a flight from norms, exemplified this trend—as well as belonging to a cohort of "girl aviators" that included Jacqueline Cochran and

Ruth Nichols, who achieved speed, distance, and altitude records.[13] Yet "lady pilots" of their reputation and esteem were rare. Working in the airline industry both expanded and reinforced gender norms, providing the prospect for women to contribute to a cutting edge industry, albeit in deferential roles that fulfilled, rather than departed from, gender expectations. Strict guidelines were submitted for hiring flight stewardesses. Boeing required that applicants weigh under 115 pounds, be no taller than five feet four inches, and be younger than twenty-five years of age. They also had to be single. In 1936 United Air Lines opened the first training center in Cheyenne, Wyoming, which formalized the professionalism of the position. However, not until the 1964 Civil Rights Act, which addressed both gender and racial discrimination, were these restrictions lifted and a semblance of parity reached with male stewards, who began to be reemployed during the 1950s.

As the longevity of flights increased through jet aircraft after the Second World War, the onboard job requirements for flight attendants also intensified. Inflight entertainment became important. With planes now carrying up to one hundred passengers, flight attendants also began to play a more significant safety role. Overall, they ascended as the primary symbol of flight experience, attending to the physical welfare and recreational pleasure of passengers, with responsibility for up to thirty passengers at a time.[14] These duties intersected visibly in terms of fashion. As touched upon previously, early airline travel was modeled after sea

FIGURE 4.6 Braniff stewardess.

travel, with "airships" and "flying-boats." This nautical approach informed the dress of flight "crew" members, which mimicked sailor uniforms and indicated a maritime vocabulary of rank, such as captain and first officer. As this fashion protocol evolved, flight route could determine style of dress. British Airways, for example, employed Indian women dressed in saris for flights to India starting in the late 1950s.[15] By 1965, Mary Wells, an advertising executive for

Braniff Airlines, contracted famed fashion designer Emilio Pucci to revamp flight attendant uniforms that accented sex appeal. "When a tired businessman gets on an airplane, we think he ought to be allowed to look at a pretty girl," Wells remarked.[16] Explaining his approach to inflight fashion, Pucci further stated, "Braniff's hostess look is chic feminine. Is simplicity and comfort and individual."[17]

This stress on fashion over function, and sex appeal in particular, was in keeping with the swinging 1960s—another case of society impinging on jet culture. The Bond girl Pussy Galore (Honor Blackman) from *Goldfinger* (1964), who is both a pilot and love interest for 007 (Sean Connery), embodied this unsteady zeitgeist of female empowerment and crass sexism. Alvin Toffler argued that this turn toward onboard luxury, inflight entertainment, and open sexual

FIGURE 4.7 *Goldfinger* (1964), directed by Guy Hamilton.

suggestion highlighted how airlines were "no longer selling transportation, as such, but a carefully designed psychological package as well."[18] Inflight fantasies could be further elaborated and attained by those with money. Hugh Hefner, publisher of *Playboy* magazine, bought a DC-9 as a private party jet during the late 1960s for an estimated $5.5 million, renaming it the Big Bunny and decking it out with a bar, cinema, and dance floor, plus showers and a fur-covered bed (jet lag be damned). The personal use and modification of private planes was not new. Frank Sinatra, who had a fear of flying due to surviving a crash in 1958, owned several planes which he used for world tours to Japan, Hong Kong, and Europe. Bars and pianos could be found onboard. His 1958 album *Come Fly with Me* helped inaugurate this new cosmopolitan jet set style.[19]

Indeed, the postwar jet age profoundly enabled celebrity culture, with stars of stage and screen now capable of traveling nationally and internationally with speed and grace in ways that had not been possible before. Acts like Elvis and Led Zeppelin had their own private jets, which rendered life on the literal road a past relic for those who had achieved superstardom. This conjuncture of technology and celebrity not only facilitated worldwide commercial reach and a new globalization but, in doing so, augmented the establishment of an American cultural hegemony similar to the way the steamship and railway had for European empires of the nineteenth century.[20]

The possibilities of sexual and other kinds of revolution through modern aviation have had their limits. Another

FIGURE 4.8 Led Zeppelin on tour, New York, 1973. Image by Bob Gruen.

intrusion of society into the world of commercial travel is the issue of race and how it exists as an unspoken theme in the history of flight. Indeed, the public sympathies that figures like Paul Bert, Filippo Marinetti, and Charles Lindbergh expressed for fascism and ideologies of racial superiority necessitate a critical vigilance about the connections between modern technologies, pseudo-scientific notions of mental aptitude, and racism. Call it another version of white flight. The legendary Tuskegee airmen and more recently the film *Hidden Figures* (2016) point to the importance of understanding the role of African-American and other minority communities in making aviation history. Another often-neglected example is Bessie Coleman, a daughter of sharecroppers who became the first woman of African-American and Native American descent to earn a pilot's license in 1921, two years before Earhart, though she had to earn it in France due to segregation.

Popular culture has cited this problem of racial lag on occasion. Jessy Terrero's film *Soul Plane* (2004)—the title paying homage to the R&B TV show *Soul Train* (1971–2006)—is a comedic sendup of the airline industry in the same fashion as Jim Abrahams and David Zucker's classic satire *Airplane!* (1980), although with a focus on race, specifically the whiteness of airline culture. *Soul Plane* builds upon an inside joke in the earlier film when a white flight

FIGURE 4.9 *Airplane!* (1980), directed by Jim Abrahams and David Zucker.

attendant (Lorna Patterson) is unable to understand two black passengers speaking jive, prompting an elderly white woman played by Barbara Billingsley—better known as June Cleaver, the mother in *Leave It to Beaver* (1957–1963)—to say, "Oh, stewardess? I speak jive." Yet *Soul Plane* also lampoons black culture from the airline name NWA (with its motto "We Fly, We Party, We Land"), to an inflight service consisting of Popeyes fried chicken and Colt 45, to an onboard restroom complete with a black bathroom attendant. There are two classes—First Class and Low Class—and instead of duty-free shopping there is onboard gambling, pole dancing, and a night club on the upper deck. Snoop Dogg reigns as the pilot in command.

Terrero's film consequently acknowledges the absence of race from conventional depictions of air culture—a

FIGURE 4.10 *Soul Plane* (2004), directed by Jessy Terrero.

presumably post-racial setting—and, in doing so, underscores the latent whiteness of this context. Like airport terminals, inflight cabins or cockpits are not immune from society. Simone Browne has examined how racism has intensified with the high-surveillance "security theater" that now characterizes airport culture post 9/11, leaving everyone under suspicion and minorities burdened especially by additional "racial baggage."[21] As with gender, the issue of race constitutes another cultural lag frequently found in commercial air travel.

A supposedly fun thing I'll have to do again

It is important to make a distinction between jet lag and exhaustion. "Fatigue to a body is like air resistance to a plane," Lindbergh writes in his account, *The Spirit of St. Louis* (1953). "If you fly twice as fast (if you continue twice as long), you encounter four times the resistance (you become several times as tired)."[22] However, as he further notes, "Elements of mind and body don't follow such clear, sharp curves of physics; they jump erratically to peaks, and back to depths, and then may strike an average for a time."[23] The science of sleep was still in its infancy when Lindbergh undertook his famed flight, though his sentiments about the correlation between speed and fatigue and the irregularity of such periods of lassitude resonate with travel conditions today. While technical advances continue apace with regard to aircraft and their abilities of distance and fuel efficiency (among other improvements), innovations have also taken hold within airline cabins to alleviate the enervation of jet travel. The experience of flight was once about the thrill of flying itself, with the purchase price paid back in the unparalleled view afforded. Though the first film screening on an aircraft occurred as early as 1925, today commercial travel can resemble a decked out living room with innumerable channels of music, films, and video games.[24] We have become even more separated from nature through these onboard distractions. Few look out the window. Like life elsewhere, we look at screens.

For those who can afford it, seating for international travel can also resemble (distantly) one's bedroom. If the airline industry has strengthened gender and racial hierarchies in certain ways, it has, perhaps above all, reinforced class differences. Journalist David Owen has reported how accommodations for inflight sleeping have become a new front for airlines seeking to lure elite passengers. Changes have not only included the fully reclining seat, but also minibars, showers, and private suites for two people—conveniences that can quickly increase a ticket price to $20,000 per person. This cost partly reflects a profit motive—first and business class seating comprise a large proportion of airline revenue—but also the expense of designing seating that is modular, lightweight, safe, and cutting edge in terms of comfort.[25]

The key aim of airlines, however, is to fill every seat and maximize the occupancy on each aircraft, resulting in a constant logarithmic accounting of seat pricing versus availability, in addition to the fine-tuned measurement of seating space in inches in order to fit as many seats on a flight as possible. Some budget airlines, such as the Irish carrier Ryanair, have pondered "standing seating" as a means of boosting capacity while ostensibly lowering costs for passengers.[26] In economy class, seating charts have become shifting topographies of short-term real estate, tagged with values of plus or minus, premium or regular, the language depending on whether a row is near the front of the aircraft or proximate to an emergency exit, promising extra legroom.[27] Websites such as SeatGuru.com and Seatmaestro.com have popped up to help passengers strategize in advance. Nonetheless, the ultimate working logic is you get what you are willing to pay for, with those with more wealth (or a lush expense account) emancipated from this class structure in the sky.

The growth of a business lounge culture at international hubs, like the one at Oliver Tambo, is another sign of this affluence and the accrued benefits of corporate loyalty. Frequent flyer programs have existed since the 1970s, and following the Airline Deregulation Act (1978), which reduced US government oversight of the industry, they have continued to blossom with ever more "rewards." Air miles have been effectively monetized through programs like MileagePlus (United Airlines) and AAdvantage (American Airlines), with travel not being an escape from work but instead being another form of production in the global economy—how far and frequently we fly generating more value by "earning" more points, even if the actual worth of such mileage rewards are miniscule fractions of a dollar, as listed in the fine print. Still, such currency can be used to purchase more tickets, hotel reservations, car rentals, gift cards, and other products and services, in addition to gaining forms of status such as Premier Gold and Premier Platinum that offer complementary upgrades, priority check-in, and early boarding. Airline credit cards, through which miles can be earned without travel, and the formation of cartels such as SkyTeam, Oneworld, and Star Alliance have further buttressed this shadow global economy, transforming vacations into a new practice of labor. Such features, while seemingly benign on the surface, indicate once more the intrusion of profit, competition, and debt into a world we like to see as an escape.

However, even airports can possess moments of rest, of contemplation, when the world seemingly falls away. After waiting for a period of almost twelve hours in the Lufthansa lounge, I boarded a South African Airways flight, only to have it cancelled due to mechanical reasons after sitting on the tarmac for an additional two hours. Led through a byzantine sequence of hallways that avoided South African sovereign territory, I slept for six hours at the airport's Protea Hotel Transit, followed by another flight that departed Johannesburg in the morning. An SAA official formally escorted me, to assure customs authorities that I had indeed

FIGURE 4.11 Washington Dulles International Airport, July 2016.

departed. After a scheduled stop in Accra, I arrived at Washington Dulles the same day, early in the evening.

I missed my connection and was unable to rebook. Incapable of securing a hotel room, I attempted to sleep in the terminal with several other passengers, first in the luggage area and later upstairs, near the ticket counters. An elderly couple, who had been on the same SAA flight with me, rested nearby, the husband a retired high school teacher from San Francisco. They had been doing some missionary work in southern Africa, exactly where I have since forgotten. Likely Botswana or Malawi. I put on my sunglasses to diminish the glare from the fluorescent lights and propped my feet on the luggage trolley, slouching in a seat to catch some rest. It is perhaps impossible to sleep deeply in an airport, but the non-time of jet lag had interceded. I thought about where I was going and where I had been, waiting for the arrival of daylight that would mean I could travel once more.

CONCLUSION: JET LAG AS A WAY OF LIFE

The future is already here. It's just unevenly distributed.

—WILLIAM GIBSON

"They are constantly on the move," Frantz Fanon writes in *The Wretched of the Earth* (1961), his classic text of Third World revolution. "The leaders and students of the underdeveloped countries are a gold mine for the airlines. Asian and African officials can attend a seminar on socialist planning in Moscow one week and then another on free trade in London or at Columbia University the next."[1] Though trained as a psychiatrist, Fanon spoke from experience in these remarks, having served as a diplomat for Algeria's National Liberation Front during that country's long anticolonial struggle against the French. He regularly flew between Tunis, Rome, Accra,

Cairo, and Bamako in this capacity before his untimely death at the age of thirty-six. Indeed, global politics has depended on such "shuttle diplomacy," to use an expression associated with former US secretary of state Henry Kissinger, a person on the opposite end of the political spectrum. Perhaps they might have agreed on this point, as well as on the hazards of jet lag. Call it a politics of unrest.

In the spirit of Fanon, this book concludes on a political note. The preceding memo-non-lectures have addressed a range of issues to position jet lag as a subject worthy of scrutiny. Jet lag gives us an alternative cultural history of globalization. It outlines a cautionary tale about our physiological relationship with technology—the latest replay of humanity's persistent Icarian ambitions. Jet lag is not wholly benign. Written against many perceptions, this book has amended popular understandings of jet lag by suggesting its deeper historical and philosophical underpinnings that lend insight into the global culture of kinesis in which we live. Jet lag is an intersectional effect of technology, time, biology, and the history of aviation. However, the latent politics of jet lag further underscore how speed has impacted contemporary life to the point that human existence as we know it is quickly receding—the ceaseless innovation of our capitalist world economy refusing to let us rest, to indulge one of our most essential human needs. This accelerationism—visually captured in Godfrey Reggio's cult film *Koyaanisqatsi* (1982)—has disrupted diurnal routines, the influence of daytime and nighttime, and the roles of leisure, contemplation, and sleep

FIGURE C.1 *Koyaanisqatsi* (1982), directed by Godfrey Reggio.

in our lives.[2] The technological enervation we once felt as being exclusive to jet travel has become commonplace. Jet lag has become a way of life.

A recent article in the Ask Well section of the *New York Times* raised an emblematic question of our age. "Is there anything I can do to train my body to need less sleep?" the reader asked, adding, "If I get less than nine hours I feel sick and exhausted the next day. (I already do the only using your bed for sleep, and not looking at screens 30 minutes before sleep.)"[3] The response to this question was negative. Dr. Sigrid Veasey, a professor at the Center for Sleep and Circadian Neurobiology at the University of Pennsylvania, advised the reader to discover their optimal sleep time, which can vary from person to person. On the other hand, an article from *Time* magazine published in October 2014 with the title "How You Can Function on Less Than 6 Hours of Sleep" offers a contrasting perspective. It recommended less TV ("This dullness is addictive."), fewer carbohydrates ("they just make me sleepy"), fewer meetings ("Blah blah blah—hate just droning on, or being droned at."), learning which hours for sleep are best ("If I can sleep from 4 to 8am, I'm very happy."), doing pleasurable things when feeling sleepy ("I hang out on Quora"), and finding a job you love ("I REALLY, REALLY, REALLY LOVE WHAT I DO."). This article appeared in the business section of *Time*.[4]

What is troubling about these pieces is not the elusiveness of an appropriate amount of sleep, but the conflicting advice on offer. Medical knowledge is placed in competition with business acumen. Physical well-being is implied as secondary to professional ambition. The initial query prompted by a desire to reduce one's time for sleep is a sign of the increasing stresses placed on day-to-day life by global online connections and technologies of instant accessibility that encourage, if not demand, sleep be reduced, that we behave more like machines. We do not have the time to do everything we need, or want, to do. "I am too busy" has become the alibi of late capitalism.

This progressively post-human environment of time scarcity resembles what Herbert Marcuse addressed in *One-Dimensional Man* (1964), a study of how the onslaught of modern consumerism has diminished human existence in advanced industrial societies. Taken further, our present is not only defined by rampant consumption, but also by a concurrent elimination of nighttime and sleep. Flows of global capital have had the effect of erosion—the erosion of time. Through noise and light pollution alike, our lives reflect the natural world less and less and the restive world of technology more and more, contributing to what art historian Pamela M. Lee has called "chronophobia" (an anxiety about time) that started during the 1960s—the jet lag decade.[5] Jet lag used to be the physical price we paid to travel with speed. Speed once gave us the "palpable sensation" of the thrill of technology.[6] Today, speed is a bargain of convenience we cannot escape.

This world has been a long time coming. The media theorist Robert Hassan has argued that political-economic empires of the past several centuries have produced simultaneously two versions of "temporal empire"—the first based on mechanized time and the second centered on information networks. These empires of time and speed have largely been invisible. Their greatest impact has been at a cognitive level, rather than manifested through borders, resource extraction, and military ventures as with visible "spatial" empires.[7] The disquieting observation Hassan makes is that the effects of these temporal empires now exceed the regulatory abilities of states. A growing "asynchronicity" exists between our neoliberal global economy and democratic political institutions.[8]

Similarly, the celebrated knowledge economy and information society that Silicon Valley and similar hubs have introduced and sustained over the past several decades highlight the financial capitalization of networking and speed over heavy industry, as noted by Jeremy Rifkin and Manuel Castells in *Time Wars* (1987) and *The Rise of the Network Society* (1996), respectively. These emergent conditions do not signal the end of industrialization as such. Rather, it has declined in places like Pittsburgh and Detroit only to relocate to Shanghai and Bangalore. To return to an earlier point, David Harvey has described the present as validating Marx's argument about capitalism's annihilation of space through time—the endless search for productive capacity and markets through increasing speed and efficiency. This trend has resulted in "the spatialization of time" whereby different places inhabit different temporalities of development and decline.[9] We live in the uneven world depicted by William Gibson in the epigraph. Innovation has incurred a variety of lags—jet lag being one among many.

These observations return to the opening of this book regarding modernity and time. Modern revolutions have ruptured and reorganized political time, as Hannah Arendt argued in *On Revolution* (1963), by auguring epochal endings and new beginnings with different timetables for democratic participation—a political landscape now being challenged by a new "dictatorship of speed" as Paul Virilio has contended, enabled by cyberspace and its temporality dependent neither on daytime nor nighttime, but only on human users who are awake and able to inhabit it.[10] It is increasingly the case that such users are willing to do so to the detriment of their own human capacity, their own bodies. Like jet lag, it is an exhaustion without labor. The dehumanization Marx warned about in the nineteenth century continues. "Was it really to 'save time' that these engines were invented?" E. M. Cioran has asked elsewhere.[11] "I seize an object, I consider myself its master," he answers, "as a matter of fact I am its slave, as I am the slave of the instrument I make, the tool I use."[12]

Though work slowdowns have long been a weapon of the weak, whether for slaves working under brutal conditions of plantation agriculture or office workers inhabiting stifling cubicles, time as a technique of dissimulation is increasingly vital. Understood properly, it can challenge modern, industrial routines organized by the twelve-hour workday, quarterly reports, and yearly cycles. It can resist the universalizing

FIGURE C.2 *Fata Morgana* (1971), directed by Werner Herzog.

effects of global capitalist time and its depletion of daily life. Unlike the non-time of jet lag, a condition that subsides, the unrest of our contemporary culture of kinesis requires a concerted effort to recover and sustain the human in the face of technology. Technology inevitably finds its own remote graveyard on the fringes of the world capitalist system, as invoked in Werner Herzog's *Fata Morgana* (1971). Yet awaiting such mechanical destiny is not enough. Restorative human action is required. "Revolution is movement," Virilio has written, "but movement is not a revolution."[13]

Infinite rest

Science fiction is an unreliable guide to the future, being primarily about the present. But it can offer an intriguing, if imperfect, glimpse of what the future might look like. The film *Alien* (1979) by Ridley Scott depicts a future not entirely unlike our present: one defined by corporate malfeasance, militarization, relentless human settlement, and encounters with life-threatening organisms. The premise of the film concerns the working-class crew of a long-haul cargo ship in deep space that responds to a distress signal, leading to the infection of a crewmember and eventually the entire ship with the titular character. Of interest here is how the plot unfolds. The crew awakens from sleep chambers in the first minutes of the film, a plausible technique of biological management backed by science, though the circumstances that arouse them turn out to be a nightmare. At the end of the film, Ellen Ripley (Sigourney Weaver), the last survivor, takes the only option left, which is to fall back asleep, with the hope that her spacecraft will be rescued at a later time. In this sense, *Alien* conforms, however tangentially, to a deeper tradition vis-à-vis sleep and its relationship to reason and unreason, as once vividly depicted by Goya. However, to be awake in this instance is be in a state of terror, to experience the absence of reason.

Andrei Tarkovsky's *Solaris* also dwells on the absence of reason, though it is not about the terrors of nonhuman species. It is about the deeply held fears of the human species—how memory and nostalgia, even when cherished, can mislead us, destabilizing our sense of reality and even repeat past trauma. Sleep in *Solaris* is not a refuge as in *Alien*, but a purgatory between different states of emotion, which leaves Kris Kelvin, and the audience, unsure about what to

FIGURE C.3 *Alien* (1979), directed by Ridley Scott.

FIGURE C.4 *Solaris* (1972), directed by Andrei Tarkovsky.

believe and pursue while awake. "That's the problem," the character Dr. Snaut (Jüri Järvet) says at one point. "Mankind has lost the ability to sleep."

These two films taken together project a set of anxieties onto the future about technology and the end of natural rhythms of human biology, the end of sleep, and the end of reason. Each is a fantasy echo of what jet lag and its wider world of technological innovation and human limitation might become.[14] The politics of rest and unrest with which this book concludes is about how the non-time of jet lag may represent a coming chronophobia, one based not on apprehensions of speed or the durational expectancy of technology, but on a complete separation from nature as we know it.[15] Jet lag in the *longue durée*, it might be said, is about our loss of contact with the celestial. Machines make emotions, whether jet aircraft or iPhones, and at an escalating pace, unlike the conditions encountered by the provisional philosophical tradition of Cervantes, Goya, Levinas, and Sartre discussed earlier.

Jet lag is instructive in this regard. Rather than solely being non-time, a "wallowing in the asphyxia of becoming" to draw once more from Cioran, jet lag can teach us to live better, more fully, through an awareness of these effects.[16] Instead of being a curse, the predicament of time being "out of joint," as Hamlet memorably confronts, can invite productive skepticism, a momentary vantage point to rethink the world, however uncertain or desperate conditions may be. As Jonathan Crary has written in 24/7, the imaginings for a better future—a less frenetic, more fulfilling one—begin with reverie, daydreams, and the respite of sleep. Sleep can serve as "a radical interruption, as a refusal of the unsparing weight of our global present."[17]

Flying also has the capacity to instill values of humanism, to encourage the sanguine possibilities of the human imagination. "To know me is to fly with me," Ryan Bingham (George Clooney), the main character of *Up in the Air* (2009), says in the film's voice-over to explain himself. "This is where I live." Bingham relishes his life in the non-places of hotel rooms, lobby bars, and airport terminals while traveling for a human resources consultancy firm. He gives occasional motivation talks with the title "What's in Your Backpack?" designed to enlighten his audience about the burdens in their terrestrial lives, the weight of responsibilities that can encumber us unduly. "Make no mistake," Bingham intones. "Moving is living."

FIGURE C.5 *Up in the Air* (2009), directed by Jason Reitman.

Nonetheless, the primary conceit of the film is that individual freedom is lonely, that weightlessness— metaphorically represented by flight—can also translate to meaninglessness, with the climax of film centered on the discovery that a kindred spirit named Alex (Vera Farmiga), with whom he develops an intimate relationship while traveling, in fact has a husband and children. His fantasy with her is permanently grounded, with the stark realization that his life has fallen short due to his shallow commitments. She symbolized a more fulfilling one. "All attachments are optimistic," Lauren Berlant has written elsewhere. "When we talk about an object of desire, we are really talking about a cluster of promises we want someone or something to make to us and make possible for us."[18] But the film refuses to condemn travel. As with many preceding stories, it facilitates self-realization, with Bingham continuing his personal airborne journey at the film's conclusion.

James Salter has similarly written of the self-knowledge gained in piloting aircraft—a connection with, rather than withdrawal from, the world. "We live in the consciousness of a single self, but in nature there seems to be something else, the consciousness of many, of all, the herds and schools, the colonies and hives with myriads lacking in what we call ego but otherwise perfect, responsive only to instinct," he describes toward the end of his memoir *Burning the Days*. "Our own lives lack this harmony. We are each of us an eventual tragedy."[19] William Langewiesche separately discusses what he calls "the aerial view"—the vantage point that flight gives us, yet we often neglect. Commercial air travel encourages us to look inward rather than outward, as mentioned before. In his words, we "draw the shades for the movie and pretend not to fly at all."[20] This amounts to a loss. "The aerial view is a democratic view," he urges.[21] What we gain from the experience of flight and looking out is that we can "see ourselves in context, as creatures struggling through life on the face of a planet, not separate from nature, but its most expressive agents."[22]

The right to travel should remain sacred and inviolable. To move is to practice freedom, to test democracy, to be human. Jet lag reminds us of our physical limits and of the Panglossian temptations of technology. But, in doing so, it can serve as motivation to appreciate, even celebrate, the role of such mortal limits and their discreet instruction. Once accepted, jet lag can present quiet hours of waking rest that allow for essential contemplation about the ethic of time and its universal lessons, while the rest of the world sleeps. Prompting us to think about the very nature of the human condition, jet lag can inspire us to grasp and fulfill the finite time we all share.

FIGURE C.6 O. R. Tambo International Airport, July 2016.

ACKNOWLEDGMENTS

This book has been an unusual project. I need to thank Chris Schaberg, Ian Bogost, and Haaris Naqvi for their enthusiastic, leap-of-faith response to my initial query. Chris's work in particular has been a source of inspiration, and I thank him for his careful attention. Katherine De Chant provided essential editorial assistance at Bloomsbury. I conducted research and wrote much of the manuscript at the Austin and Boston Public Libraries, as well as Widener Library at Harvard. I thank the staff at each for their assistance. I also worked on it as a visiting scholar with the Committee on Globalization and Social Change at the CUNY Graduate Center and while a writer-in-residence in the Frederick Lewis Allen Room at the New York Public Library in 2016; my thanks to Gary Wilder and Melanie Locay for facilitating these opportunities. I would like to acknowledge Bob Gruen and various museum and archival staff for their assistance in the licensing of images used in this book. The research of R. E. G. Davies, Keith Lovegrove, Richard Hallion, and Victoria Vantoch informed much of the historical background outlined in this project, more than the endnotes convey. Lafayette College provided publication funding. Friends, colleagues, and audiences who helped and allowed me to digress (at length) on jet lag include Rob Blunt, Greta Brubaker, Lindsay Ceballos, Caleb Gallemore, Ellie Gamble, Rachel Goshgarian, Gabrielle Hecht, HIST 105 (Fall 2016), Andy Ivaska, Constantin Katsakioris, Charles Piot, and Josh Sanborn. Sarah Duff read every chapter with a keen eye. Though short, I would like to dedicate this book to my mom, who gave me a working title and, along with my dad, taught me the essential skill of travel.

LIST OF ILLUSTRATIONS

Introduction

Chapter 1

Chapter 2

Chapter 3

Chapter 4

Conclusion

NOTES

Introduction

1 Pico Iyer, "The Uninvited Guest," *New York Times*, December 27, 2007. Available online: http://jetlagged.blogs.nytimes.com/2007/12/27/the-uninvited-guest/ (accessed February 1, 2017).

2 Don DeLillo, *Mao II* (New York: Viking, 1991), 23.

3 Patrick Smith, *Cockpit Confidential: Everything You Need to Know About Air Travel, Questions, Answers & Reflections* (Naperville, IL: Sourcebooks, 2013).

4 Kathleen Stewart, *Ordinary Affects* (Durham, NC: Duke University Press, 2007), 2, 3.

5 Lauren Berlant, *Cruel Optimism* (Durham, NC: Duke University Press, 2011), 24.

6 Pico Iyer, *The Global Soul: Jet Lag, Shopping Malls, and the Search for Home* (New York: Knopf, 2000), 85.

7 Bruno Latour, *We Have Never Been Modern*, trans. Catherine Porter (Cambridge, MA: Harvard University Press, 1993), 51–55, 142–45.

8 Bill Brown, *A Sense of Things: The Object Matter of American Literature* (Chicago: University of Chicago Press, 2004), 4.

9 See Graham Harman, *Towards Speculative Realism: Essays and Lectures* (Ropley, UK: Zero Books, 2010); Steven Shaviro, *The Universe of Things: On Speculative Realism* (Minneapolis, MN: University of Minnesota Press, 2014).

10 Arianna Huffington, *The Sleep Revolution: Transforming Your Life, One Night at a Time* (New York: Harmony, 2016).

11 Edward Tenner, *Why Things Bite Back: Technology and the Revenge of Unintended Consequences* (New York: Vintage, 1997), 6.

12 E. M. Cioran, *The Fall into Time*, trans. Richard Howard (Chicago: Quadrangle Books, 1970 [1964]), 177. It should be noted that Cioran's concerns in this book focus on the differences between religious and secular time

13 Henri Bergson, *Key Writings*, eds. John Mullarkey and Keith Ansell Pearson (London: Bloomsbury, 2002), 159.

14 Martin Heidegger, *Being and Time*, trans. John MacQuarrie and Edward Robinson (New York: HarperCollins, 2008 [1962]), 429.

15 Miguel de Cervantes, *Don Quixote*, trans. Edith Grossman (New York: HarperCollins, 2003), 21.

16 Goya and Hegel were commenting on a period of counterrevolution and the limits of the Enlightenment, as witnessed with the Reign of Terror and the rise of Napoleon.

17 Emmanuel Levinas, *Time and the Other*, trans. Richard A. Cohen (Pittsburgh: Duquesne University Press, 1987), 48. Unlike wakefulness, insomnia could also result in "depersonalization" and object-hood. See Emmanuel Levinas, *Existence and Existents*, trans. Alphonso Lingis (Pittsburgh: Duquesne University Press, 2001), 66.

18 Thomas Pynchon, "The Deadly Sins/Sloth; Nearer, My Couch, to Thee," *New York Times*, June 6, 1993. Available online: https://www.nytimes.com/books/97/05/18/reviews/pynchon-sloth.html (accessed February 1, 2017).

19 Mark Vanhoenacker, *Skyfaring: A Journey with a Pilot* (New York: Vintage, 2016), 224.

20 Italo Calvino, *Six Memos for the Next Millennium* (Cambridge, MA: Harvard University Press, 1988); e. e. cummings, *i: six nonlectures* (Cambridge, MA: Harvard University Press, 1991 [1953]).

21 Roland Barthes, *Mythologies*, trans. Annette Lavers (New York: Hill and Wang, 1972 [1957]), 71.

Chapter 1

1 John Tresch, *The Romantic Machine: Utopian Science and Technology after Napoleon* (Chicago: University of Chicago Press, 2012), xi.

2 Rebecca Solnit, *The Faraway Nearby* (New York: Penguin, 2014), 32.

3 Milan Kundera, *Slowness*, trans. Linda Asher (New York: HarperCollins, 1996), 2.

4 Wolfgang Schivelbusch, *The Railway Journey: The Industrialization of Time and Space in the Nineteenth Century* (Berkeley: University of California Press, 1986).

5 Walter Benjamin, *Radio Benjamin*, ed. Lecia Rosenthal, trans. Jonathan Lutes, Lisa Harries Schumann, and Diana K. Reese (London: Verso, 2014), 172.

6   Paul Theroux, *Riding the Iron Rooster: By Train Through China* (Boston: Houghton Mifflin, 2006 [1988]), 15.

7   Italo Calvino, *Six Memos for the Next Millennium* (Cambridge, MA: Harvard University Press, 1988), 39.

8   William Langewiesche, *Inside the Sky: A Meditation on Flight* (New York: Pantheon Books, 1998), 3.

9   James Salter, *Burning the Days: Recollection* (New York: Vintage, 1997), 141.

10 Richard P. Hallion, *Taking Flight: Inventing the Aerial Age from Antiquity through the First World War* (New York: Oxford University Press, 2003), 52–53.

11 Ibid., 29–30.

12 Ibid., 53–54.

13 Paul Virilio, *Speed and Politics: An Essay on Dromology*, trans. Mark Polizzotti (Los Angeles: Semiotext(e), 2006 [1977]), 90.

14 Thomas Pynchon, *Against the Day* (New York: Penguin, 2006), 25.

15 Ibid., 4.

16 R. E. G. Davies, *Airlines of the Jet Age: A History* (Washington, DC: Smithsonian Institution Scholarly Press, 2011), 1.

17 Ibid., 11–12.

18 Ibid., 6.

19 W. G. Sebald, "Reflections: A Natural History of Destruction," *New Yorker*, November 4, 2002, 70–71.

20 Mark C. Taylor, *Speed Limits: Where Time Went and Why We Have So Little Left* (New Haven, CT: Yale University Press, 2014), 6.

21 E. M. Cioran, *The Fall into Time*, trans. Richard Howard (Chicago: Quadrangle Books, 1970 [1964]), 73.

22 Martin Heidegger, *The Question Concerning Technology and Other Essays*, trans. William Lovitt (New York: Harper & Row, 1977), 4.

Chapter 2

1 David Harvey, *The Condition of Postmodernity: An Enquiry into the Origins of Cultural Change* (Cambridge, MA: Blackwell, 1990), 202.

2 Martin Heidegger, *Being and Time*, trans. John MacQuarrie and Edward Robinson (New York: HarperCollins, 2008 [1962]), 469.

3 Lewis Mumford, *Technics and Civilization* (Chicago: University of Chicago Press, 2010 [1934]), 14.

4 Eviatar Zerubavel, *Time Maps: Collective Memory and the Social Shape of the Past* (Chicago: University of Chicago Press, 2003).

5 Daniel Rosenberg and Anthony Grafton, *Cartographies of Time* (New York: Princeton Architectural Press, 2010), 54–56.

6 Ibid., 19–20.

7 Mumford, *Technics of Civilization*, 14.

8 Dava Sobel, *Longitude* (New York: Bloomsbury, 2007 [1995]), 79.

9 Ibid., 78.

10 Vanessa Ogle, *The Global Transformation of Time: 1870–1950* (Cambridge, MA: Harvard University Press, 2015).

11 On Barak, *On Time: Technology and Temporality in Modern Egypt* (Berkeley: University of California Press, 2013), 5.

12 Peter Galison, *Einstein's Clocks, Poincaré's Maps: Empires of Time* (New York: Norton, 2004), 13, 278.

13 Ibid., 325.

14 Jimena Canales, *The Physicist and the Philosopher: Einstein, Bergson, and the Debate that Changed Our Understanding of Time* (Princeton, NJ: Princeton University Press, 2015).

15 Jimena Canales, *A Tenth of a Second: A History* (Chicago: University of Chicago Press, 2009), 13.

16 Karl Marx, *Grundrisse: Foundations of the Critique of Political Economy*, trans. Martin Nicolaus (New York: Penguin, 1973), 524, 539.

17 Johannes Fabian, *Time and the Other: How Anthropology Makes Its Object* (New York: Columbia University Press, 2002 [1983]).

18 Walter Benjamin, *Illuminations: Essays and Reflections*, ed. Hannah Arendt, trans. Harry Zohn (New York: Schocken Books, 1968 [1955]), 261–62.

19 His emphasis. E. M. Cioran, *The Fall into Time*, trans. Richard Howard (Chicago: Quadrangle Books, 1970 [1964]), 176.

Chapter 3

1 Till Roenneberg, *Internal Time: Chronotypes, Social Jet Lag, and Why You're So Tired* (Cambridge, MA: Harvard University Press, 2012), chapter 2.

2 William Gibson, *Pattern Recognition* (New York: Penguin Putnam, 2003), 1.

3   Bruce Chatwin, *The Songlines* (New York: Penguin, 1988), 230.

4   Johannes Fabian, *Time and the Other: How Anthropology Makes Its Object* (New York: Columbia University Press, 2002 [1983]).

5   Georges Gurvitch, *The Spectrum of Social Time*, trans. Myrtle Korenbaum (Dordrecht, Holland: D. Reidel, 1964), 31.

6   Judith Fein, "Emotional Jetlag: Do You Suffer From Emotional Jetlag?" *Psychology Today*, June 30, 2014. Available online: https://www.psychologytoday.com/blog/life-is-trip/201406/emotional-jetlag (accessed February 2, 2017).

7   Don Quixote is mentioned in the original novel by Stanislaw Lem, but not these lines specifically.

8   As quoted in Rosamond Kent Sprague, "Aristotle and the Metaphysics of Sleep," *Review of Metaphysics* 31, no. 2 (1977): 230.

9   Alberto Cambrosio and Peter Keating, "The Disciplinary Stake: The Case of Chronobiology," *Social Studies of Science* 13 (1983): 329.

10 Jonathan Crary, *24/7* (London: Verso, 2013), 3.

11 Roenneberg, *Internal Time*, 43.

12 As quoted in Enda Duffy, *The Speed Handbook: Velocity, Pleasure, Modernism* (Durham, NC: Duke University Press, 2009), 17.

13 Lawrence Rainey, et al., eds., *Futurism: An Anthology* (New Haven, CT: Yale University Press, 2009), 51, 283–86.

14 Duffy, *The Speed Handbook*, 19.

15 Roland Barthes, *Mythologies*, trans. Annette Lavers (New York: Hill and Wang, 1972 [1957]), 71.

16 Martin Amis, *Money: A Suicide Note* (London: Jonathan Cape, 1984), 249.

17 Joanna Klein, "Why Jet Lag Can Feel Worse When You Travel From West to East," *New York Times*, July 15, 2016. Available online: http://www.nytimes.com/2016/07/16/science/jet-lag-east-west.html (accessed February 2, 2017).

18 Steve Hendricks, "The Empty Stomach: Fasting to Beat Jet Lag," *Harper's Magazine*, March 5, 2012. Available online: http://harpers.org/blog/2012/03/the-empty-stomach-fasting-to-beat-jet-lag/ (accessed February 2, 2017).

19 Tracie White, "Study finds possible new jet-lag treatment: Exposure to flashing light," *Stanford Medicine, News Center*, February 8, 2016. Available online: https://med.stanford.edu/news/all-news/2016/02/study-finds-possible-new-jet-lag-treatment.html (accessed February 2, 2017).

20 Rebecca Maksel, "When did the term 'jet lag' come into use?" *Airspacemag.com*, June 17, 2008. Available online: http://www.airspacemag.com/need-to-know/when-did-the-term-jet-lag-come-into-use-71638/ (accessed February 2, 2017).

21 George T. Hauty and Thomas Adams, "Pilot Fatigue: Intercontinental Jet Flight" (Federal Aviation Agency, Office of Aviation Medicine, Oklahoma City, 1965), 1.

22 Franco Moretti, "The Dialectic of Fear," *New Left Review* I/136 (1982): 67–85.

23 Zora Neale Hurston, *Tell My Horse: Voodoo and Life in Haiti and Jamaica* (New York: HarperCollins, 2009 [1938]), 179.

24 Reinhart Koselleck, *Futures Past: On the Semantics of Historical Time*, trans. Keith Tribe (New York: Columbia University Press, 2004 [1979]), 11.

Chapter 4

1 Alvin Toffler, *Future Shock* (New York: Bantam Books, 1971), 217.

2 Alain de Botton, *A Week at the Airport: A Heathrow Diary* (London: Profile Books, 2009), 29.

3 James Clifford, *Routes: Travel and Translation in the Late Twentieth Century* (Cambridge, MA: Harvard University Press, 1997), 3.

4 George Santayana, *The Birth of Reason and Other Essays*, ed. Daniel Cory (New York: Columbia University Press, 1968), 5.

5 Alastair Gordon, *Naked Airport: A Cultural History of the World's Most Revolutionary Structure* (Chicago: University of Chicago Press, 2008 [2004]), 44.

6 On nostalgia, see Christopher Schaberg, *The End of Airports* (New York: Bloomsbury Academic, 2015).

7 Marc Augé, *Non-Places: An Introduction to Supermodernity*, trans. John Howe (London: Verso, 2008 [1992]), xviii.

8 Sarah Sharma, *In the Meantime: Temporality and Cultural Politics* (Durham, NC: Duke University Press, 2014), 29.

9 Paul Virilio, *Pure War* (New York: Semiotext(e), 1997), 77.

10 Augé, *Non-Places*, 70.

11 Ibid., 89.

12 Guy Debord, *Society of the Spectacle*, trans. Ken Knabb (London: Rebel Press, 2004 [1967]), 14.

13 Victoria Vantoch, *The Jet Sex: Airline Stewardesses and the Making of an American Icon* (Philadelphia: University of Pennsylvania Press, 2013), 12, 13.

14 Keith Lovegrove, *Airline: Identity, Design and Culture* (London: Laurence King, 2000), 17.

15 Ibid.

16 As quoted in Ibid., 22.

17 As quoted in Ibid., 24.

18 Toffler, *Future Shock*, 224–25.

19 William Stadiem, *Jet Set: The People, the Planes, the Glamour, and the Romance in Aviation's Glory Years* (New York: Ballantine Books, 2014), 3–4.

20 Jenifer Van Vleck, *Empire of the Air: Aviation and the American Ascendancy* (Cambridge, MA: Harvard University Press, 2013), 14, 120.

21 Simone Browne, *Dark Matters: On the Surveillance of Blackness* (Durham, NC: Duke University Press, 2015), 27, 28.

22 Charles A. Lindbergh, *The Spirit of St. Louis* (New York: Scribner, 2003 [1953]), 218.

23 Ibid.

24 Lovegrove, *Airline*, 81.

25 David Owen, "Game of Thrones," *The New Yorker*, April 21, 2014. Available online: http://www.newyorker.com/magazine/2014/04/21/game-of-thrones (accessed February 2, 2017).

26 Frances Cha, "Coming soon? Standing instead of sitting on planes," CNN.com, July 10, 2014. Available online: http://www.cnn.com/2014/07/10/travel/standing-cabin-plane-study/ (accessed February 2, 2017).

27 Tim Wu, "Why Airlines Want to Make You Suffer," *The New Yorker*, December 26, 2014. Available online: http://www.

newyorker.com/business/currency/airlines-want-you-to-suffer
(accessed February 2, 2017).

Conclusion

1 Frantz Fanon, *The Wretched of the Earth*, trans. Richard
  Philcox (New York: Grove, 2004 [1961]), 42.

2 On accelerationism, see, for example, Benjamin Noys, *Malign
  Velocities: Accelerationism and Capitalism* (Alresford, UK:
  Zero Books, 2014).

3 Karen Weintraub, "Ask Well: Can You Train Yourself to Need
  Less Sleep?" *New York Times*, June 17, 2016. Available online:
  http://well.blogs.nytimes.com/2016/06/17/ask-well-can-you-
  train-yourself-to-need-less-sleep/ (accessed February 2, 2017).

4 Alexandra Damsker, "How You Can Function on Less Than 6
  Hours of Sleep," Time.com, October 28, 2014. Available online:
  http://time.com/3544255/function-little-sleep/?xid=tcoshare
  (accessed February 2, 2017).

5 Pamela M. Lee, *Chronophobia: On Time in the Art of the 1960s*
  (Cambridge, MA: MIT Press, 2004).

6 Enda Duffy, *The Speed Handbook: Velocity, Pleasure,
  Modernism* (Durham, NC: Duke University Press, 2009), 273.

7 Robert Hassan, *Empires of Speed: Time and the Acceleration of
  Politics and Society* (Leiden: Brill, 2009), 2–3.

8 Ibid., 11.

9 David Harvey, *The Condition of Postmodernity: An Enquiry
  into the Origins of Cultural Change* (Oxford: Blackwell, 1990),
  205, 273.

10 Paul Virilio, "Speed and Information: Cyberspace Alarm!" Ctheory.com, August 27, 1995. Available online: http://www.ctheory.net/articles.aspx?id=72 (accessed February 2, 2017).

11 E. M. Cioran, *The Fall into Time*, trans. Richard Howard (Chicago: Quadrangle Books, 1970 [1964]), 67.

12 Ibid., 68–69.

13 Paul Virilio, *Speed and Politics: An Essay on Dromology*, trans. Mark Polizzotti (Los Angeles: Semiotext(e), 2006 [1977]), 43.

14 Joan W. Scott, "Fantasy Echo: History and the Construction of Identity," *Critical Inquiry* 27, no. 2 (2001): 284–304.

15 On durational expectancy, see Alvin Toffler, *Future Shock* (New York: Bantam Books, 1971), 42.

16 Cioran, *The Fall into Time*, 174.

17 Jonathan Crary, *24/7* (London: Verso, 2013), 128.

18 Lauren Berlant, *Cruel Optimism* (Durham, NC: Duke University Press, 2011), 23.

19 James Salter, *Burning the Days: Recollection* (New York: Random House, 1997), 349–50.

20 William Langewiesche, *Inside the Sky: A Meditation on Flight* (New York: Pantheon Books, 1998), 6.

21 Ibid., 9.

22 Ibid., 4.

INDEX

Page references for illustrations appear in *italics*.